With very best wishes -
many thanks for all your
help in College Chapel

# ROYLE EXCHANGE

### Roger Royle

Hodder & Stoughton
LONDON SYDNEY AUCKLAND TORONTO

**British Library Cataloguing in Publication Data**
Royle, Roger
  Royle exchange.
  1. Great Britain. Radio programmes. Broadcasting
  I. Title
  791.44092

ISBN 0-340-40739-5

Published by Hodder and Stoughton,
a division of Hodder and Stoughton Ltd,
Mill Road, Dunton Green, Sevenoaks, Kent TN13 2YA.
Editorial Office: 47 Bedford Square, London WC1B 3DP.

Typeset by Hewer Text Composition Services, Edinburgh.
Printed in Great Britain by Clays Ltd, St Ives plc.

# DEDICATION

I would very much like to dedicate this book to all those who have worked with me on *Good Morning Sunday* and especially Michael Wakelin, Hilary Mayo, Tanya Astley, Jenny Pitt, Rosemary Foxcroft and Alison Jones, who were the very faithful and friendly team who saw me right through to the end. And last, but by no means least, Doris Probert, a very faithful listener.

# FOREWORD

Writing this book has brought back very many memories for me – most of which are extremely happy ones. I have, in the main, concentrated on *Good Morning Sunday* because I feel that programme was so much part of my life, but in a book of this sort it is impossible to capture everything about a programme or even the tremendous amount of work that many people, some of whose names are rarely heard on air, put into it. But to them all I would like to express my thanks.

I have used verbatim transcript, off air, to recall the many fascinating meetings I have had with some very interesting people. But as you will gather, when you read, people do not always speak in well-constructed sentences – but I thought it was better that you read what they said rather than my sanitised version. We did, however, remove a few of the um's and er's.

The typing of this book has been a mammoth undertaking which would not have been achieved had it not been for the very hard work of Barbie Carthew and Jenny Pitt. Sue Jones, Jean Godfrey and Iris Monteverdie also came to my rescue when yet more transcripts had to be produced. Keeping an eye on my style has been the ever-helpful eye and discerning pencil of Hilary Hunt. And a thank you also goes to John and Candis Roberts, Andrew and Anna, who allowed me to hide away in their house.

For those situations and people I have not been able to include in this book I apologise. What is included I hope you will greatly enjoy.

# CONTENTS

# GETTING THE GUESTS

'My eight-twenty guest is . . .' For the past five years that phrase was ingrained in my mind as I used it regularly on my Radio 2 programme *Good Morning Sunday*. The format consisted mainly of dedications and records but each week there was a special guest. The idea of timing the guest was drawn from John Dunn who always announced his 'After Seven' guest in a similar way. It was important for me to say who was coming up right at the start of each edition of *Good Morning Sunday* because this was one way of attracting people to go on listening to the programme. It was also a way of trying to make sure that people didn't leave me for their local radio stations, since these often started their religious broadcasting after the eight o'clock news.

However, the interval between announcing and actually introducing the guest was often long and difficult. The final decision was the producer's but the main work was done by the researcher. Every six or eight weeks we would have a *Good Morning Sunday* meeting of everyone who worked on the production side of the programme. These meetings normally took place over a BBC lunch. Now I know the BBC canteen is much maligned but they used to do us proud. There is no shortage of delicate sandwiches, and if you were into quiche or crumbed chicken legs your taste buds were tantalised. Fortunately they always provided fruit as an alternative to the calorie-infested gateau which was always on the menu by special request. We did try a few breakfast meetings but they didn't prove too popular – I wonder why?

At each meeting the performances of the guests on the previous programmes were discussed. Obviously views differed. Some were thought to have had little to say; some had survived because they had been edited well; usually the majority were thought to have delivered the goods. In the main, guests were well-known names with something to say about their faith. Normally that faith was Christian but it certainly didn't have to be. One thing I did learn was the very widely differing views people had about such things as prayer, sin and life after death.

Once the past guests had been reviewed we set about making suggestions for future programmes. It was here that personal likes and dislikes came to the fore. I have to confess it was very early on that I suggested Shirley Bassey – not because I thought she had a deep faith or a strong theological mind – but because I longed to meet her. Some of the listeners very quickly saw through this, but I thought that now and again there was no harm in my having a little treat. Tanya, one of the production assistants, longed to meet the singer Don Francisco. He was far easier to justify than Shirley. He has got a deep faith which he is always willing to talk about and we played his records on the programme.

Although we were fortunate to have both the Duke of Edinburgh and the King of Tonga on the programme, we always hoped for another Royal. Our very first choice was always the Queen Mother but this was purely a pipe dream as she doesn't give interviews. Sadly, during my time it proved impossible to get either the Prince of Wales or the Duchess of Kent, both of whom we all wanted. It would be difficult to get a Royal, we realised, partly because the BBC has very strict rules about asking for such interviews. Not only do you have to go through BBC procedures, you also have to get through the Palace Guard, and I can tell you that neither is an easy touch.

Politicians were regularly listed as possibles. Here again there were pitfalls. Three times we tried to get Mrs Thatcher but failed. Personally, this was a great disappointment partly because she has quite a lot to say about the Church and the Christian faith and partly because I think it would have been good for her to have the opportunity to talk as a person rather than as the Prime Minister.

However, had Mrs Thatcher appeared we would obviously have had to ask Neil Kinnock. This may not have been easy as he is a declared atheist! But doubtless he would have been able to give his reasons for not believing in God and this could well have been very interesting. With politicians balance is essential. If you have one from the Right you must have one from the Middle or the Left. Very early on I realised that the programme was being monitored for political bias. The political parties make it their job to listen out for any ways in which they feel that they may be being undermined or shown in an unfavourable light. Mind you, there are times when I believe their sensitivity gets the better of them and they see trouble where no trouble is. *Good Morning Sunday* is in no way a party political broadcast. Politicians are interviewed because they have a faith and are willing to talk about it, and not because they need a boost to their profile or to plug their latest campaign or hobby-horse. Most of them heard our warnings and behaved extremely well.

During the free-for-all at the *Good Morning Sunday* meetings, when names were being submitted, obvious notice was taken of who might be 'in town'. This was a good way of trying to catch up with visitors to this country so giving the programme an international feel. Dr Billy Graham and Archbishop Desmond Tutu were just two of the visitors who accepted our invitation. Neither was easy to engage as their arrangements were often in the hands of others who had compiled very full diaries for them. But once they were tracked down they were well worth having.

On one occasion, I remember, we caught up with Billy Graham in his hotel. It was obvious that a day had been given over to the media. Along with other members of the world's press and broadcasting organisations I waited in an ante-room for my name to be called. Once it was called we were ushered into The Presence. The engineer had to set up the equipment and we had to get down to work straight away. Dr Graham was charming but I had the feeling that both he and I were on a conveyor belt and neither of us was saying anything new.

The second time I interviewed him things were very different. He kindly consented to come to Broadcasting House in London and this time I felt that I got a much better interview. I wasn't so overawed and he wasn't under such pressure. Mind you, the way he manages to stay so calm under such high demands is a sure sign of the steadfastness of his faith and the strength he gets from prayer.

With Archbishop Tutu it was a different ball game. He had appeared on the programme once before, by telephone from South Africa. That Christmas Day we did a programme of lessons and carols with leading Christians reading the lessons. At a pre-arranged time I telephoned the Archbishop to wish him a Happy Christmas and to ask him what he wanted for his country for Christmas. The reply was just one word – 'Hope'. He then, fortunately, expanded on his wish as one word interviews do not, on the whole, make good broadcasting. His talk held no party political comment. However, the very fact that he was on the programme on Christmas Day made one MP very angry, and in his anger he wrote to the Controller of Radio 2 to complain. Fortunately, the Controller showed me the letter so I was able to deal with it. The way in which I did this I shall tell you later. Having made his comment about Hope, the Archbishop read the story of the shepherds in St Luke's Gospel and the telephone call came to an end.

The time I interviewed Archbishop Tutu in London was not without problems. It was at a time when the Archbishop was much sought after by the media and quite a lot of the reporting was far from friendly. We had to meet up with him in his hideaway in South London where he was staying with the family of one of his godchildren. The journey was well worth the effort and we came away with a quality interview, showing the Archbishop in a very different light from the image some have of him purely as a political agitator. This was truly a Father-in-God speaking.

Because of his Jewish faith, Barry Manilow was also someone we hoped to interview and the head of Religious Broadcasting's secretary, Jackie, even volunteered to give up some of her own free time to help. I think somehow she had been caught up by the Manilow Magic. However, both she and I were thwarted. Mr Manilow doesn't give interviews.

The names of old favourites had a habit of reappearing at several meetings. Thora Hird could always be relied upon to be a good guest and it was great that she was prepared to become a friend of the programme, and certainly she was someone the listeners never tired of hearing. The man who made 'Order, order' into a national catchphrase was much sought after and extremely co-operative – Lord Tonypandy, George Thomas. He was even generous enough to allow us to interview him in hospital. It was at the time when he was fighting his battle against serious illness but this didn't stop him from allowing us to go to his bedside at St Thomas's Hospital and to do the interview there. It was fortunate that I knew the Sister in charge of the ward but I'm sure this had nothing to do with us gaining access. George's lilting Welsh voice is a joy to hear and what he has to say about his faith is always said with conviction and sincerity.

And then of course there's Cliff – Cliff Richard. He is only a year or so younger than I am but he has weathered a good deal better. As a performer he has earned the respect of a very wide cross-section of people. At a time when it was not fashionable for people in the pop world to talk about their faith Cliff was prepared to come clean. And he has remained faithful ever since. It is also now a faith strongly linked with good works. His connections with the Christian relief agency, Tear Fund, has shown that his faith is not, for him, a private matter concerned with saving his own soul. It is a realisation that St James was right when he said that faith without works is dead.

Every so often we went to America in search of big stars. Many Americans are very up front about their faith but catching them for an interview is another matter. I had only just taken over presenting *Good Morning Sunday* when the first trip to the States occurred. These trips were always very exhausting, involving not only a good deal of travelling but also a great element of uncertainty. Obviously, before we left we had certain names booked but we always hoped to get more once we arrived so that the trip could be cost effective. This was easier said than done. Americans seem to lead a life of perpetual motion. They are very difficult to tie down. There was always a great sigh of relief when you did manage to get through to the star's agent but this was only one step along the road. Often they would say they would call back to make the necessary arrangements. But words and actions are two totally different things. On one occasion Judith, one of the researchers, spent a whole day waiting by a telephone for it to ring; it didn't despite her devotion to duty.

Another hazard is being offered a guest you know little about. This happened with one Californian individual. This actor was playing a leading role in a television soap opera which was very popular on both sides of the Atlantic. We were only told that we could interview him as we finished doing another interview. The producer, John Forrest, and I travelled on to meet the interviewee while Judith went off in search of more information. The situation wasn't helped by the fact that neither John nor I watched that particular soap. Had he been in *Coronation Street* I would have had no difficulties whatsoever. Soon after we arrived at the house Judith telephoned with the information. Under cover of John's general questions about the weather, the arrangements for the next day and telephone calls from the United Kingdom, Judith was able to give him all the information that she had been able to get on the interviewee. John made some hasty notes and found a way of handing them surreptitiously to me. The interview took place. It turned out to be quite a good one and I don't think the interviewee ever realised that originally we hadn't a clue as to who he was.

Some guests were not, of course, big names at all. Few people will have heard of Jean Vanier or Kerena Marchant but they certainly had a story to tell, and from the letters that I received afterwards what they had to say was much appreciated by the audience. There is a great danger in programmes like *Good Morning Sunday* to think that you must always have star names. Yes, people are extremely interested in the person behind the star and they are only too pleased to hear about their thoughts and their beliefs – stars were rarely invited to plug books, shows or records on *Good Morning Sunday* – but there are a tremendous number of people who are doing such worthwhile things who are very rarely heard about. Many of these people are gleaned from outside broadcasts – I think of the WRVS, the Pilsdon community, the bellringers of East Devon, and many others whose faith is the driving force behind their actions.

This, of course, is true about the people interviewed on *Songs of Praise*. Only once then do I remember interviewing a star, if you don't count the Roman Catholic Archbishop of Liverpool, and that was in Holmfirth. It is in this beautiful Yorkshire town that the television series, *Last of the Summer Wine*, is filmed, so it was thought only right that a member of the cast should be included in the programme and who better than Kathy Staff, or Nora Batty as she is known to millions. In all the glory of her wrinkled stockings she talked about her faith and the fact that she sang in her own church choir.

Holmfirth has become something of a tourist attraction and on the Sunday when I did the interview there were several coach loads of tourists all hoping to get a glimpse of their favourite star. Autograph hunters were well to the fore and one young lad seeing me standing alongside a cameraman thought I must be a star so kindly asked me for my autograph. He then looked at what I had written and said, 'Roger Royle, well who are you?'

Having decided who you wish to interview, the problem is then persuading them to be interviewed. Some you can telephone directly, but with the vast majority you have to go through their agents and secretaries, many of whom make guard dogs look like playful puppies. It is the researcher who has this difficult and very time-consuming task. Fortunately, I was privileged to work with very good researchers who were determined to catch their prey. With some people it meant going to their homes or where they worked, and although this obviously took time, it was often worthwhile as you felt that you knew more about someone in their natural surroundings.

Mary Whitehouse very kindly invited me into her home. It was exactly as I would have expected. It was very much a family home, filled with flowers, pleasant and comfortable despite the activity going on within it. Tony Benn's home was an eye-opener. He and his wife made us extremely welcome and offered us cups of tea and coffee immediately on arrival. He has a most amazing collection of miners' lamps and recordings of all his broadcasts and articles are filed in his basement. The home also wasn't short of musical instruments. One home in which there was obviously a piano was the London home of Edward Heath. This seemed to be very much a working home and apart from a quite animated discussion about the memorial service for the late Sydney Evans, a former dean of Salisbury, it was a matter of doing the interview and leaving. It was a real privilege to visit an actress that I have greatly admired for a long time – Dame Judi Dench – in her home. She lives in a small cottage overlooking a cemetery in North London and in some ways it seemed as though she was in the middle of the country, but this fascinatingly beautiful cottage home just seemed to reflect the tremendous talent of both Dame Judi and her husband Michael Williams. One home it was a real treat to visit was the home, in Sussex, of Malcolm and Kitty Muggeridge. Malcolm was a writer and wit that I have always respected, even if sometimes I have disagreed with him. But to see these two elderly people together, still very much in love, was so refreshing. The sadness was to see how Malcolm's eyesight was failing but he had an extra pair of eyes in Kitty. They couldn't have made us more welcome and we were loath to leave, especially as it meant eating our last piece of Kitty's cake, which was sheer delight. It was no wonder that a few years later we visited them again.

Generally people are prepared to have a radio crew back again because, on the whole, radio causes little upset in their home; but wise people think twice before inviting television even once. By the time lights, cameras and microphones have been put into position, you wonder whether you're still in charge of your own home. However, with years of experience most television crews put things back where they found them.

Even so, as you leave a home, having done a television interview, you can sense the relief on the interviewee's face as the invading army retreats and they try to return to normal.

The vast majority of *Good Morning Sunday* interviews were done in the studio and were nearly always recorded ahead of time. This meant that mistakes could be removed and the whole interview, if necessary, trimmed to time. Time is the all-powerful god when it comes to broadcasting. I soon realised that if I crashed the pips at eight o'clock, or overran my ending time at twenty seconds to nine, I would experience Judgment Day then and there. Although it is very good to be disciplined by time it can also be a very restricting force. People are not immediately relaxed the moment they come into a studio. In fact, the opposite is generally true. I would try to spend time getting to know the guest and letting the guest know me but this was impossible if we were doing several interviews back to back. Then either you or they had to be off to another appointment, or the studio was in constant use so that lingering was not allowed.

One of the ways in which I tried to relax my guests was to tell them that it would be a Sunday morning breakfast chat. I always told them that the interview wouldn't be confrontational, nor would I be out to trick them. With members of the general public I generally told them that we could always do it again if we got anything wrong and this certainly eased the strain. By reassuring the guests that I wouldn't trick them it meant that quite often we got a far better interview. They were prepared to trust and as far as I know there was only one guest who later regretted what she had said – and that was the American singer Donna Summer. Prunella Scales did ring back to check that what she had said was all right.

Many interviews these days are very confrontational and as interviewer and interviewee say good morning to each other, you feel that it's through gritted teeth, preparing to do battle. In some ways I believe that this means we now find out far less about people than we used to. Any politician or person in the public eye with any sense these days makes sure that they are properly trained to face interviewers. Much money is made from these training courses. But it means that instead of

9

getting the truth we get what the interviewee wants us to know, and that's not always the same thing. And you are left with an interviewer who has become angry and frustrated.

I have always maintained that we, as the general public, do not have the right to know everything about a public figure's private life and thoughts. If they wish to share them with us then that, I believe, is their prerogative and not our right. I remember one of the most moving radio interviews I ever did was in the Rover's Return, which is part of the *Coronation Street* set at Granada Television Studios, Manchester. The actor, William Roache (or, as he is better known in 'The Street', Ken Barlow) was willing to talk about how he and his wife Sarah reacted to the death of their daughter, Edwina. Although I had read about this tragic situation in the papers and magazines it was a tremendous privilege to hear William himself talking about it. I also felt it was a sign of his great generosity. It is never easy to talk about something that is so personal, but William realised that by expressing his feelings and his faith he would be helping others, which he certainly did.

I once interviewed a gentleman, sadly now dead, who had been a patient in the Royal Berkshire Hospital in Reading before moving to a Leonard Cheshire Home in Nettlebed, Oxfordshire. He, very kindly, was willing to be interviewed on *Songs of Praise* and to talk about the care he had received from the medical profession; it was a programme for St Lukestide. He also talked about the wonderful support he had received from his wife and then, after I had asked him, from others. As he started to tell me about the various people in different parts of the country who were remembering him in their prayers he burst into tears. My immediate reaction was to get out of my seat to comfort him and to get between the camera and him so that no more filming could take place. Seeing someone in tears may make good television but I didn't wish to be part of something which failed to respect someone's privacy.

None of the interviews I did, whether for radio or television, was done without proper research with which I was always well supplied. These notes were gathered either by talking to the person direct or with their agent. If they had written their autobiography that could be a real mine of information. The BBC keeps an excellent reference library and from it it was possible to gather press cuttings about the interviewee. However, I soon learned how to tread carefully where press cuttings were concerned. There were times when they were barely based on the truth and the stories that were built around them bore scant resemblance to what had actually happened or been said. At times, though, they were very helpful indeed as they gave me insight into a person's character which helped to make the interview more interesting. Some interviewees would tell the same story time and time again. I felt it was then important to try and find something new to talk about. One of the hardest things for the researcher to do was to find out anything about the interviewee's faith. It was, of course, obvious with people like Thora, Cliff, Dana, Wendy Craig or the Archbishop of Canterbury, but with many of the other stars it was not so obvious. Sometimes all we were able to find out was that they had been educated by nuns or had played the clown in a nativity play and on this we hoped to build.

At times some interviewees talked more positively about their faith than we could possibly have hoped for. Others seemed to have views which were very much their own and were light years away from what might be regarded as orthodox teaching. This was certainly true in conversations that I had with many about life after death. Sometimes it was a matter of using every skill in the book to get them to say anything about their faith even though all were told what sort of programme *Good Morning Sunday* is. By asking a singer if they saw their unusual skills as being a gift from God, or asking someone who had been through difficulties whether they'd looked to God for support, I was generally able to establish something about their faith – but I do remember two interviews where I failed completely. At the end of one I still wasn't sure whether the interviewee was a Jew or a Roman Catholic and another person told me that he thought a piece of prose called *Footsteps*, which many people find uplifting, was written by St Paul to the people of Corinth.

*11*

With the number of guests that had to be found for both the regular programmes and the special outside broadcasts it was obvious that now and again some details about a person might be a little inaccurate. This happened in Austria where I was doing the programme for Christmas Day. A couple of days before Christmas we pre-recorded a piece about Mozart at his birth place in Salzburg. I was fortunate enough to get Dr Leonore Haupt-Stummer, an expert in his work, to talk about his music. We had been unable to find out very much about Professor Leonore herself, but I did have two pieces of information. The first was that she was the only person allowed to play Mozart's piano, and the second was that she had played for our Queen when she had made an official visit to that majestic city. Our research was 100% wrong: other people are allowed to play Mozart's piano and she played for Prince Charles and not the Queen.

# THE PRAYER SLOT

Eight-twenty may well have been the time that my main guest appeared on the programme but earlier there was another important guest who came into the studio to do what we called, for purposes of convenience, 'the prayer slot'. It was always live and consisted of a three-minute written piece followed by a short conversation. Originally this item was genuinely a prayer slot, as listeners were asked to write either with the names of people and situations to be prayed for as well as their favourite prayers. The Right Reverend William Westwood was the bishop who handled this slot for a long while. Known to the listeners as Bishop Bill, he would create an oasis of peace and reflection which was greatly appreciated by many of the listeners. But when I became the presenter of the programme things changed. My predecessor was Paul Macdowell, a layman, but with me being ordained it was felt that there should be a slight change of emphasis. The only rule that was laid down by the Controller of Radio 2 was that the cleric doing the prayer slot should be someone senior to me. This sort of person was not difficult to find as at the time I was a non-stipendiary minister licensed to the Bishop of Southwark – you can't get very much lower than that! The person was not always a member of the Church of England and sometimes wasn't a Christian.

Included in the team of prayer slot presenters was Rabbi Hugo Gryn who was very popular. I was very pleased to work with him as I had known him for some time. He frequently came to Eton to lecture and I remember inviting him once to speak during Christian worship on how he, as a Jew, saw the person of Jesus. At no time did he lose his own integrity as a Jew and yet in no way was he offensive to the Christians who were listening to him – and this can't have been easy. I also have great respect for Rabbi Hugo because he had first-hand experience of very deep suffering and yet he is not bitter. His family had suffered greatly at the hands of the Nazis in Auschwitz and this experience has obviously left its mark, but also from it came strength to understand the suffering that others experienced.

He would often be on the programme at the times of Jewish feasts or fasts and this enabled him to teach non-Jews the meanings of these occasions. But to Christians it also gave greater insights to those events which were very much part of the life of Jesus and from which Jesus drew some of his spiritual strength.

As a Rabbi, Hugo is a great teacher and in the teaching tradition of the rabbis he would always make great use of stories. One particular story I remember is the one he told me at the beginning of 1990:

Like most people – I, too, have been thinking about time – how it flows in from the eternity that is behind us – how it washes over us before moving towards that eternity that lies ahead. And how – in all of God's creation – we humans are the only creatures who measure and count time. To be sure trees get a new ring every year – and horses get longer and longer in the tooth (and for that matter so do I!) – but we seem to be the only ones to whom it matters and who are so conscious of the passage of the years.

As I listened to the chimes of Big Ben at midnight a week ago – and for good measure to the Greenwich time signal on the radio as well, which gave seven – not six! – pips because last year was a whole second longer (yes, Roger, it isn't just you and me – the whole world is slowing down!) – I remember a story told me by my grandfather so long ago and far away.

About a remote village in Carpathia which had all the

necessary produce and services for ordinary everyday life – except for one thing. Its one and only watchmaker died or moved away, and there was no one to take his place. And as this happened in the pre-electronic microchip era, before very long none of the clocks and watches was accurate. Some became slow, some gained, some gave up the ghost altogether. Most people gave up on their timepieces as well, they put them in drawers or consigned them to attics, forgotten – they just rusted away. But some people kept winding their watches and faithfully oiled their clocks even if they could not rely on them. And then, one day, an itinerant watchmaker came to the village. Everyone rushed to him, but he could only repair and set right the ones that were kept going. The others were just so much junk!

During the closing and dramatic months of the year that is gone – as I watched the crumbling wall in Berlin – the throngs of people in Timisoara and Bucharest – and especially the students and their teachers in Czechoslovakia – such unpredictable and hope-filled events – and the promise that this final decade of our tragic century may signal greater harmonies, I thought 'how wonderful that these people did not neglect their spiritual timepieces. They did not throw away their ideals, nor did they give up on their dreams.'

The Bishop of Stepney, the Right Reverend Jim Thompson, became the main contributor to this slot. Known as Bishop Jim he had the added advantage of having a horse, a dog and a cat. Every so often we would have updates on the health and welfare of these animals and I can assure you that there is nothing that warms the hearts of an audience more than news about animals. On one occasion Jim used a lovely story about his dog, Jake, to illustrate a point that he wanted to make:

Early Friday morning I was taking Jake – our springer spaniel – for a walk in the park. A great gust of wind whipped my beautiful new cap, given to me by my sister for

Christmas – soaring away like a frisbee, into the lake. There it was, circled by coots and swans. I was hatless and helpless. But I had a brainwave – Jake loves swimming and springers are bred to retrieve – so I pointed towards the cap, and I said 'Fetch it, fetch it'. At which point he went into a frenzy of enthusiasm, and leapt into the water. Unfortunately, although he knew I needed assistance, he had no idea what I wanted to be fetched – so he swam round and round in feverish circles. 'Fetch my HAT' I shouted, patting my bald head, 'OVER THERE'. Imagine my delight when he paddled towards the cap, the swans and coots scattered and my dynamic dog surged up to the hat, swam round it, and came back with enthusiasm, but without the hat.

The next ploy was to throw sticks onto and around the cap so that it might suggest that my frantic shouts and sign language were not unconnected with the now sodden and sinking headgear. But it was no use, he kept on fetching the sticks and dropping them obediently at my feet. I thought 'The dog is not the way, I'll wait for the prevailing wind'. Ten minutes later I picked my cap out of the water on the far side of the lake, with a happy and bedraggled helper at my side.

He had enthusiasm, a strong desire to help, but he could not see what I needed. I sympathise because I know just what that's like. Vicars are meant to be helpful, indeed all Christians are called to be Good Samaritans, but sometimes, however much we want to help, we can't see what is needed.

Bishop Jim has a gift which few possess. He is able to speak to audiences on both Radio 2 and Radio 4. I was once told by a producer that I had too great a Radio 2 image to be suitable to do Radio 4's *Thought for the Day* but Jim can manage both extremely well. He is also a Christian who believes that the Gospels speak to all sorts and conditions of men and women in every situation of life. This meant that his scripts would have great everyday relevance. It also meant that on occasions he had to change his script at the last moment because of what had happened on the Saturday. This was certainly true the night of the infamous Poll Tax Demonstration in London in 1990. He had written a script which was suitable for Passion Sunday, preparing the listeners for the most sacred time in the Church's year. But with the tremendous disturbances and riots that had taken place on the Saturday evening he felt it was important for him to make some Christian comment on the situation. As the programme began he was putting the finishing touches to his script. It was the lead story in the news that morning and we would have been very irresponsible as Christians not to have made some comment upon it. This did, however, cause a few difficulties. Whenever a Christian, and especially a bishop of the Church of England, makes some comment about something in the news he is accused of either dabbling in politics or showing a party political bias. All scripts were vetted by the producer of the day to make sure that there was no party political bias but this didn't stop people seeing, or rather hearing it. Most of the accusations were both abusive and unfair. Tremendous trouble was taken to make sure a balanced picture was created, but then if something is against the teaching of the Gospel it is the duty of a Christian, and especially a bishop, to say so. It has to be remembered that Jesus in his day was open to the accusation of bias.

In the chat that we had after the person had spoken it was possible for me at times to play devil's advocate. I could put the other point of view especially if it was something controversial, so that the listeners of all shades of opinion could feel that their voice was being heard.

It was very appropriate that from the newspaper church, St Bride's in Fleet Street, we had, as one of our prayer slot contributors the rector, the Reverend Canon John Oates. This connection with St Bride's started with the beginning of the Choirgirl of the Year competition. St Bride's were kind enough to act as host for the final of that competition. But there was also another advantage to being linked with St Bride's. The church had become a special place of prayer for the British hostages in the Middle East, especially the journalist John McCarthy. And John Oates regularly submitted a prayer to the *Sunday Express* for the hostages which, of course, included Terry Waite, the Archbishop's envoy, and John McCarthy. With the many stories that were being put out about the hostages in the newspapers it was very useful to have someone on the programme who could keep us, as much as possible, in touch with the real situation. Often there was very little to report as most of the stories were based on rumour. However, many of the listeners kept the hostages in their prayers and it was only right that these prayers should be as well informed as possible and that the families of the hostages knew that we hadn't forgotten them in their suffering.

Very often John Oates ended his talk with a prayer and without fail it meant that there were scores of letters asking for a copy of that prayer. Certainly I realised the emphasis that many of the listeners put on prayer by the number of prayer cards that they kindly sent me. I should think that, of all the prayers used on *Good Morning Sunday*, the one by Henry Scott Holland about death was the most sought after.

## DEATH IS NOTHING AT ALL

Death is nothing at all . . . I have only slipped away into the next room . . . I am I and you are you . . . whatever we were to each other, that we are still. Call me by my old familiar name, speak to me in the easy way which you always used. Put no difference into your tone, wear no forced air of solemnity or sorrow. Laugh as we always laughed at the little jokes we enjoyed together. Play, smile, think of me, pray for me.

Let my name be ever the household word that it always was. Let it be spoken without effect, without the ghost of a shadow on it. Life means all that it ever meant. It is the same as it ever was, there is absolutely unbroken continuity . . . What is this death but a negligible accident? Why should I be out of mind because I am out of sight? I am just waiting for you, for an interval, somewhere very near, just around the corner . . . All is well.

*Canon Henry Scott Holland*

I shouldn't really have been surprised that that piece attracted such a response. With so many of the listeners being bereaved it was only natural that they should respond to something which offered such positive comfort.

On the very first morning that I became the programme's regular presenter the prayer slot was done by a woman. She was the Reverend Mother of a nunnery from Seville in Spain in whose garden I was presenting the programme. It was Easter morning and, naturally, she was very busy. At the time that we went on air she was nowhere to be seen. Obviously I was very nervous – it was a real baptism by fire. You can't afford a programme to go wrong at any time but you certainly can't make a mess of your first one, especially when it's an overseas broadcast and it's Easter Day! Fortunately, just before she was due to speak she arrived, walking in the garden in the cool of the morning. I breathed a sigh of relief and thought that the Lord, and the Reverend Mother, were on my side.

During my time with *Good Morning Sunday* there was only one woman who started to appear regularly on the prayer slot. She was none other than the General of The Salvation Army, General Eva Burrows, who one morning, by mistake I called *Dame* Eva Burrows but, as listeners to the programme would know, mistakes come very easily to me.

General Eva is from Australia and her beautiful Australian voice made for very easy listening. She had originally been on the programme as the eight-twenty guest, but because of the way she spoke and the things she had to say and her position within The Salvation Army, we very much wanted her back. The Salvation Army is held in high esteem in this country and people who often have little time for churchgoers have great respect for members of The Salvation Army. Because of General Eva's commitments throughout the world we were sadly unable to have her on the programme as frequently as we would have liked, but when she was free we made a beeline for her.

General Eva also knew the importance of using stories to attract the attention of the listener and to make a point. One I distinctly remember is this story:

I heard about one woman who was hectically busy buying Christmas presents and all the food needed for the Christmas celebrations, when she suddenly realised she had forgotten to send Christmas cards to her friends. So she dashed out to a stationery shop and, seeing a Christmas card with a nice picture, she said 'I'll have 40 of those'. She hurried home and soon had them posted off. A couple of days later she was looking at the few cards that still remained. What a shock she received when she actually read the verse in the card which she had not even noticed before. It said:

> This card comes just to say
> A little gift is on the way.

So all those disappointed friends are still waiting for that promised gift.

Fortunately, it wasn't like that with God's promised gift to the world. He kept his promise. Long, long ago the Jewish prophets spoke and wrote about that promised gift. Like the prophet Isaiah who said, 'Behold a virgin shall conceive and bear a son and his name shall be Immanuel – God with us.'

When we were doing an outside broadcast it wasn't always easy to find someone to do the prayer slot. First of all, it was essential that they could speak clear English. It's not easy to put subtitles up on radio, or even have simultaneous translation! They also needed to be people who were not frightened by a microphone or a Radio 2 audience. These people were not easy to find. Even in this country, when we were broadcasting from such places as Bath, Bournemouth, Bognor, Blackpool, Bradford, Scarborough, Whitby, Cardiff, Glasgow or East Devon, we had to search for the right person. They, of course, had no trouble with the language. It was the style that some found difficult. However, we thought it important that the person doing the pieces should be an indigenous native rather than an imported BBC regular. On most occasions it worked very well indeed. I remember one Christmas working very hard with a priest in Salzburg to make sure that his script was right. Fortunately, he wasn't one of those priests who will not accept help, he was only too ready to take advice and in the end both the contents and the delivery of his script were very good. In Whitby it was quite easy because the Bishop of Whitby is a Radio 2 regular, but some of the clergy in the other places had had very little broadcasting experience. However, most came through the ordeal with flying colours.

At one time *Good Morning Sunday* had homes in cities other than London. It came regularly from Manchester and from Bristol. Every other week I would either head north or west to present the programme from one or other of these regional centres. Manchester I know quite well as both my parents came from that area and I still have relatives living nearby. Bristol has always been a city that I've liked; it seems to have everything – music, theatre, beautiful countryside and is only minutes away from the sea. The problem was being able to find the right place to stay. In both places I had several moves before I finally found somewhere peaceful to lay my head.

Once again, it was local people that we used for the prayer slot. In Manchester it was the Bishop of Stockport, the Right Reverend Frank Sargeant. To my knowledge he had had no previous broadcasting experience but he was willing to learn. Both his and Jim Thompson's wife are called Sally, but it seems that the bishops' leisure interests are very different. With Frank I enquired about his painting rather than his animals, and I'm pleased to say that despite the fact that we gave him a child's colouring book once as a present, he gave me one of his original water colours which now hangs happily in my house.

It was good to have a northern input into the programme and by many of the illustrations that he used, Frank made people more aware of life north of Watford:

Last Monday, Bank Holiday, my boys decided that Sally, my wife, and I needed a change. They decided that we should go to Blackpool for the day – the attraction being a new ride (the Revolution) they hadn't tried and just to prove they meant it they got up early enough to go. A holdup on the motorway was enough to cast doubt upon the wisdom of the trip – shall we go somewhere else? Who wanted to go anyway? Eventually, we got there but I'm told that the best marriages are strained in traffic jams!

It was a glorious day with a stiff sea breeze. The tide was in and the waves threw themselves against the sea wall, high into the air and then showered those walking on the prom, much to their delight.

There was an air of celebration. People of all ages – wearing bright spring colours – were enjoying being out and being together. All day I didn't hear anyone shout at anyone else unless in laughter. The latest in seaside fun are tinsel wigs that make people look like sparkling Cleopatras.

It was good to be there, but into the experience came memories. The memory of going to Blackpool the day before our eldest son left home to go to university. That was the beginning of the breakup of our total family, which we have to expect. But it's a marker in family life. There was the memory, too, of walking up and down the prom with my father, the year after mother died, and how he, in turn, remembered their holidays and the good times of their early married days.

And it struck me as the memories and the waves came cascading down that our Christian lives depend upon the twin abilities of remembering and celebrating.

Bristol posed very few problems when it came to finding someone for the prayer slot. Within the Church of England Diocese of Bristol, there was someone who knew the BBC studios in Whiteladies Road far better than I did. The Bishop of Malmesbury, the Right Reverend Peter Firth, had been the Head of Religious Broadcasting in the south west for a long time. Former colleagues were very pleased to see him back in the studios. Peter knew both sides of the microphone well, both as a producer and presenter so he was able to fit into the demands of the job with little stress. However, this doesn't mean that he found the job easy. Writing a three-minute script is very difficult indeed. You can waste neither time nor words. It has to sound conversational and relaxed and must also capture the interest of the audience in the first few seconds. And it needs a powerful punchline. Ecclesiastical jargon or empty cliches will not do. The teaching has to be simple and direct and at the same time it must not be trivial or patronising. It's a tall order and even when you have taken the very greatest care, and watched every word that you've used, you find people hearing what they want to hear rather than what you actually said. But I do maintain that, on the whole, radio listeners listen with greater care than do their fellow citizens who watch the television. Television watchers are far more likely to get the wrong end of the stick.

Peter showed his strengths as a broadcaster with such scripts as this:

Christians talk about turning the world upside down, but it takes a lot of hard work and a lot of unselfishness to make a happy family or a peaceful world. I've always liked the story – that Dolly Parton has now put into a song – about the little boy who'd helped a lot in the home one day and at the end of it he presented his mother with a bill which read: 'For washing up 3 times at 5p a time – 15p. For going 2 errands – 10p. For cleaning out my bedroom – 20p. Total – you owe me 45p.' And when he went up to bed that night, he found a little note under his pillow which read: 'For feeding and clothing you for 13 years; for mending 87 socks and 17 shirts; for nursing you through measles, mumps, German measles, chicken pox and innumerable coughs and colds; for washing up for 13 years after a thousand meals – minus 3 – for catering and entertaining for 13 birthdays and for 10 seaside holidays: total bill – nothing. You owe me nothing.'

That's what it takes to turn the world the right way up – the hard work of love, which is beyond price.

On one occasion the Roman Catholic Bishop of Arundel and Brighton, the Right Reverend Murphy O'Connor, was persuaded to join us, one Sunday in Advent. He began his talk with a lovely story:

I seem to have spent quite a lot of time these past few weeks in just waiting – waiting for trains at Victoria Station, waiting for telephone calls, or waiting for someone to turn up, a kind of anxious waiting. It reminds me of the parish priest who said to his people one Sunday: 'Dear people, I have very sad news for you this morning. The bishop has decided to move me from the parish and I must leave very soon. But don't be too upset because the bishop has promised he will send a very good man in my place.' After the service, the priest went outside and saw two ladies weeping. He said to them: 'Don't be so upset that I am leaving. Didn't I tell you that the bishop has promised he will send somebody good in my place?' 'Oh yes, Father,' one of them said, 'but he said that last time!'

Although the prayer slot was rarely short of humour, neither was it short of teaching or provocative thought. Often it received a very interested response from the listeners. To me it represented something which the listeners could really get their teeth into and for those who were housebound it provided them with a thought for the week.

# LET'S CELEBRATE

The major festivals of the Christian year called for special programmes – so special in fact that on Radio 2 I was allowed an extra half-hour at Christmas. Obviously, they were also special on *Songs of Praise* but I never felt as strongly about them as I did about the radio programmes, mainly because of course *Songs of Praise* was recorded well before the event. One *Songs of Praise* recording I shall never forget was for a Palm Sunday programme from Liverpool's Metropolitan Cathedral. This was recorded on a Saturday a couple of weeks before Christmas. On the Friday night Cliff Michelmore had been in the Cathedral recording a programme for Epiphany. As soon as he had finished the poinsettias were removed and the palms were put into place. They had to be removed after our recording so that the Cathedral could then go back again into Advent. It's difficult to capture the special atmosphere under these, albeit necessary, conditions.

I have other memories of that programme. All the interviewees were young people and a delightful bunch they were too, especially a young chap who was not ashamed of his Christian faith even though many of his friends made fun of it. We interviewed him in his front room at home. The house was terraced with a front door leading into the lounge and the lounge leading into the kitchen. For some reason, unknown to me, we were doing the recording at the time when the rest of the family were returning for their tea. We would just start to film when the front door would open, another member of the family would arrive, say excuse me, clamber over the settee and make their way to the kitchen and their tea. It made for quite a lengthy, but very enjoyable, interview.

But that was nothing in comparison with the recording of a *Songs of Praise* for Christmas in Wells Cathedral. I have never ceased to be amazed at the patience of *Songs of Praise* congregations who will sing their hearts out for three and a half hours so as to make a thirty-five minute programme. And this often after having had a full-blown rehearsal the previous evening. On that particular evening in November, just before Remembrance weekend, we spent about three hours recording one carol, 'Once in Royal David's City'. The director wanted the carol sung in procession through the cloisters into the Cathedral. For added beauty the choir carried lighted candles but no allowance had been made for the November winds. It was a long time before it was possible to get a shot which included each and every candle burning brightly.

With radio it is different. The programme was nearly always live. Many people listen to *Good Morning Sunday* on their own and so, by being live, you are really keeping them company, which is a great way of celebrating Christmas. The first Christmas Day broadcast I did was from Bethlehem. In some ways this was not quite as mystical as I had hoped it would be. Manger Square on Christmas Eve leaves a lot to be desired. The actual programme was coming from a home for disabled children run by Edmund Shehada.

Bethlehem is not without tension and some of the forty-three children in the home had suffered severely as a result of the troubles. They had physical disabilities mostly, from polio and cerebral palsy to spina bifida. But despite their difficulties, they were very bright happy children.

I had arrived several days before the programme so that the children could get to know and trust me. I taught them to say Merry Christmas in English and together we learned 'Jingle Bells'. The staff of the home were totally dedicated and Leonard Cheshire, who had connections with the place, recorded a special goodwill message for us. The programme started with me on a donkey travelling the streets of

Bethlehem. For this opening sequence I'd written a short script. The donkey with its two young keepers duly arrived. They were wanting fun rather than work and the moment I mounted the donkey they smelled my nervousness. The boys encouraged the donkey to go at a rather fast pace and while I remonstrated with them the hope of making a recording went completely by the board. Eventually order was restored and the recording was made. What was not realised at the time was that donkeys in Bethlehem have no shoes so there was no nice clip-clop sound under my speech. This was rectified when the programme was broadcast because as the tape of talking was transmitted a sound-effects disc of a well-shoed donkey was played.

The donkey was not the only problem that we faced on Christmas Day. The engineers had done a great job in linking the children's home with a maternity home not far away. This was so that we could have news of the first baby born in Bethlehem that Christmas morning. Just as the news came through we sadly lost the connection so the producer, Hugh Faupel, insisted that we got the midwife to us as soon as possible. She arrived just before I was about to play the last record. I chatted merrily about the baby but I didn't have time to ask her the child's name. It was just as well. He was called Mohammed – which wouldn't have been ideal for a Christmas Day programme.

Bethlehem was a natural place to choose for Christmas, but other places also had to be found to tell the story of the real meaning behind the festival. The White Horse Inn in St Wolfgang in Austria turned out to be a very imaginative choice. This programme also began with me travelling but this time on a horse-drawn sleigh. There was no need for sound effects with this recording. The only thing we lacked was the snow that should have been Deep and Crisp and Even. Many of the holidaymakers in the hotel which had, of course, been made famous through the musical of the same name, were British. It was natural that the programme took on the atmosphere of a Christmas morning breakfast party. Inserted into it were recordings that we had made previously. On Christmas Eve I had visited the small village of Oberndorf for a special service which commemorated the writing of the internationally famous carol 'Silent Night'. Written by the local priest and the schoolmaster, it was originally performed by two men with guitar and a choir. To get the story of the carol I talked to Dr Friedrick Lepperdingere:

**RR**   Tell me about this little chapel that we're in.

**FL**   Well, it's the Silent Night Chapel, a memorial chapel, and it stands in the place of the original Silent Night Church which was dedicated to St Nicholas. But it took them about ten years just to finish this small chapel dedicated to the memory of the two creators of the song 'Silent Night'. There are two glass windows showing the two creators – one is showing Josef Mohr and the other Franz Xavier Gruber.

**RR**   Tell me about Josef Mohr.

**FL**   Well, Josef Mohr was an Assistant Priest. He came to Oberndorf in 1817, post-war time, the war of Napoleon was over – a very poor time. The people didn't have enough money to repair the broken organ of St Nicholas and so Josef Mohr asked his friend, a schoolteacher of Arnsdorf, to write music to his poem which he had written just before Christmas 1818, and Franz Xavier Gruber wrote some music for a tenor and a bass.

**RR**   So they could sing it together.

**FL**   Yes, yes, and Josef Mohr said he wanted to play the guitar with it. On Christmas Eve it was usual, it's still usual, to go to church and to have some music with the Mass. But there was no organ, and so during Midnight Mass they performed the song for its first time and it was quite a surprise for the people because suddenly fine music was to be heard from the choir-room. So the song 'Silent Night, Holy Night' came into existence, and it spread from here all over the world.

**RR**   So it was originally written to cheer the people of Oberndorf up?

FL     Yes. Well, it was just an easy way to make some cheer.

RR     In the Christmas midnight.

FL     Yes, that's right.

RR     How did it travel out though, because it never remained within the village itself, did it?

FL     The people liked it very much and so the song became some sort of folk song. A year or two later, an organ mender from Tyrol came to Oberndorf to repair the broken organ, and he heard about this Christmas song. He took the song back with him to Tyrol and from there it spread. Ten years later it was sung in Berlin and it was the Prussian Court who enquired where it came from. By enquiring in Salzburg, they found out it was Josef Mohr and Franz Xavier Gruber who were the song's creators.

Austria is, of course, the home of Mozart and *The Sound of Music*. Professor Leonore Haupt-Stummer told me about Mozart and his music:

RR     What sort of religious music did Mozart write?

LH     Mozart, particularly in the time when he was still in Salzburg, wrote much music for the church – many masses, because of course he was employed as of his thirteenth year by the Prince Archbishop of Salzburg. And so in the different Salzburg churches much of Mozart's church music was played.

RR     Now did he just write this music because he was employed to do it or did he have a religious feeling himself?

LH     Well, I think that certainly there was the impetus that he was asked to compose masses here, it was very important of course that he did that, and later when he lived in Vienna, like in the last years of his life – when he came back to Salzburg – he composed the C Minor Mass for St Peter's which his wife would sing the soprano part and then his last work – the Requiem – which maybe now brings your question if he was a religious person that his last work would be a Requiem.

**RR** But he was very young when he died, wasn't he?

**LH** Yes, he was only thirty-five years old.

**RR** And what sort of a person was he?

**LH** I think that he was extremely lively, and, at the same time very deep and very spontaneous and he could be extremely happy and jump over chairs, but then he would much, much of his time was dedicated to composing, even if he wouldn't write, the compositions would work in him.

**RR** And his music means a tremendous amount to you?

**LH** Of course. Not only to me, but I think to the whole world.

She also very kindly played two pieces on Mozart's own piano, a great treat because, as I mentioned before, the Professor is one of the few people allowed to play the instrument. The story of *The Sound of Music* is known to most of us, mainly because we have had the opportunity to see the film many times on television. But it was interesting to hear what effect the film had on Salzburg. The most fascinating story of the programme for me was the story of St Wolfgang himself. In my ignorance I am afraid I had little or no idea as to whom this gentleman was. Franz Zimmerman enlightened me:

**RR** He was living as a hermit on his own.

**FZ** In a hermitage yes. And very often he was seduced by the Devil.

**RR** It has never happened to me, but I am told people are seduced by the Devil!

**FZ** So, one day God told him he should throw an axe as far as he could and on the place where the axe fell he had to build a church.

**RR** And how many miles did he throw it?

**FZ** Four and a half miles!

**RR** That's not bad. So he was a good axe-thrower.

FZ   He was the right man for the book of records.

RR   We mustn't mention a word like 'Guinness' here.

FZ   No, no, I didn't! He found the axe on the rock which is now in the middle of the church in St Wolfgang, and he started to build the church. But he was not as strong as was necessary, and so the Devil came and asked if he could help him. St Wolfgang said, 'Of course, of course, will you help me?' The Devil replied, 'Yes I will, but you must give me a promise . . .'

RR   It's always the same with the Devil, it's always the same.

FZ   St Wolfgang said, 'What is the promise? What do I have to do?' The Devil answered, 'As soon as the church is ready, the first living being that enters the church is mine.' And so when the church was perfectly finished St Wolfgang didn't enter the church because he knew how dangerous this would have been.

RR   So who went in instead?

FZ   A wolf. A young wolf came and went into the church and the Devil, hidden behind the door, took this animal. As soon as he noticed that this was an animal he became so angry that he went through the ceiling and out from the church. You can still see the hole – the black hole in the ceiling of the church of St Wolfgang.

Being away for Christmas (or Easter) meant members of the team being separated from their families. This was a lot to ask of anyone. So often, as soon as the programme was over, we would make for the nearest airport. After we had finished the programme in St Wolfgang, Hilary Mayo, Michael Wakelin, Jenny Pitt, who had had rather a difficult Christmas Eve – having got locked in her hotel bedroom – and I drove hell for leather to Vienna to catch the only available plane. Very few people were travelling so we had plenty of space. What we lacked was celebratory food. One open sandwich each was a sad substitute for a traditional family Christmas meal.

We were certain of a white Christmas when in 1989 we went to Lapland. The Hotel Pohjanhovi, from which we did the programme, was very well heated but outside the temperatures were at a steady minus twenty-four degrees centigrade and descending. Several recordings had to be made prior to the programme, in the great outdoors. Heavily clad in my thermals and a thickly quilted anorak I set off with the team, similarly attired, to record a reindeer-sleigh ride. Rudolph couldn't be found so I was landed with Pilki. Like all animals, Pilki had a mind of his own but at least nothing disastrous happened. Well not on the sleigh. The disaster occurred when at the end of the ride, I was invited into a typical Lapp tent and entertained with a special Koskenkova Finnish drink. It was like having your own in-built central heating. The only trouble was it hit the back of the throat with such force that it became extremely difficult to speak coherently.

As well as the snow, Lapland obviously supplied me with Father Christmas. Here, I was told, was where Father Christmas lived. It is here that post addressed to Father Christmas is delivered from all over the world; and it is from here that the replies are sent. I was allowed, with the help of Outi, one of Father Christmas's elves, to look through his vast postbag. Many children had written from Britain. Trying to make a brief joke I pretended that the Right Reverend David Jenkins, the Bishop of Durham, had written to Father Christmas adding, as an aside, 'but I didn't think he believed in Santa'. This raised the wrath of one listener who pointed out to me that he had found it far easier to understand the Bishop of Durham than he did many of the traditional Christian teachers. I took the reprimand.

The one thing that I found difficult to believe was the fact that there were two Father Christmases, one for ordinary mortals and the other for those who flew in by Concord at about £1,400 a head.

If Bethlehem was ideal for Christmas, Jerusalem was a natural for Easter. The programme was based at the St Andrew's Hospice, a Church of Scotland hostel overlooking the south-west corner of the Old City and the Church of the

Last Supper. Always aware of the need for balance we recorded interviews at both the Garden Tomb and the Church of the Holy Sepulchre.

At the Garden Tomb Peter Wells told me of the traditions that lay behind that site:

**RR** It was in a garden that Mary first met the risen Lord, and so it's to a garden – a very special garden to many Christians – that I've come. It's the Garden Tomb which is just outside the Old City of Jerusalem, and with me is the General Secretary of the Garden Tomb Association, Peter Wells. Peter, a very happy Easter to you.

**PW** And a happy Easter to you, Roger, and welcome to the Garden Tomb.

**RR** Now I believe this is associated with General Gordon?

**PW** Yes, that's right. In about 1870 or so, General Gordon and many others thought that the site of the crucifixion was very close to here on a hill just along the path there, and they were therefore looking in this area for a tomb. In fact in 1860 or thereabouts, a Greek was digging for a water system around this garden and he came across the solid rock of the tomb. Of course, it was too much hard work digging through there so he put the rubble back and left it. It was later on that General Gordon and others came to see the tomb and wondered – some were indeed convinced – that this was the tomb in which Jesus was buried.

I visited the Church of the Holy Sepulchre on the one day in the year when it was normally closed to visitors, as it was the day that the Blessed Sacrament was exposed in the sepulchre itself. I had visited the church many times before but on this particular occasion it was extremely special. It had become a house of prayer, rather than a tourist site. The significance of its being the central shrine of Christianity for many Christians came home to me then. Although I still find it difficult to come to terms with the way in which it represents divided Christendom.

Father Theophilus was my guide:

RR I have now come inside what many people believe to be the holiest place on earth – the Holy Sepulchre – the probable site of Christ's crucifixion, burial and resurrection, and I'm standing on the rock of the crucifixion – Golgotha – with a member of the Greek Orthodox Patriarchate, Father Theophilus. Father Theophilus, good morning to you.

FT Good morning.

RR How long ago was it discovered?

FT It goes back to the fourth century when the mother of Emperor Constantine, Helena, came over here and undertook all these excavations and restorations.

RR And I believe at this altar here we have a very holy site indeed. Can we kneel down and try to look inside.

FT Yes, I can show you with candles. According to tradition this was the actual place of the Cross itself, and next to it we can see the cracks of the rock.

RR Where the lightning struck?

FT Right. Yes.

RR That is amazing. Well, there's another very holy place here because there's the empty tomb as well, downstairs. But we've got to get down there first. Can we go down those stairs over there? Now there are mainly chapels in this church, aren't there? So there are lots of Christians who are worshipping here regularly. Which churches do they actually come from?

FT The Holy Sepulchre is shared, we can see, by three major Christian communities.

RR Yes.

FT The Greek Orthodox, the Latins and the Armenians, as well as by three ancient Eastern churches, the Assyrians, the Copts and the Abyssinians.

**RR**    And how do you get on, all you different churches together?

**FT**    Everything has been arranged in such a way and there is a place, I mean space, and time for everybody.

**RR**    Father, if we just walk towards the entrance of the empty sepulchre. How important is the empty sepulchre to you?

**FT**    Extremely important, because the very culmination of Christian faith, of the mystery of the incarnation, is the Resurrection and the emptiness of the tomb is the strongest testimony, the strongest proof of Christ's Resurrection. Christianity is not an origin as people try to describe it. It's the truth, and I think it's only Christ himself who says and claims that 'I am The Truth'.

When visiting Jerusalem it is easy to get caught up with the traditions that have been passed down through the ages. The need was to try and see them in a new light. Father Jerome Murphy O'Connor, a biblical scholar based in Jerusalem, provided me with a new insight to the Via Dolorosa, the Way of Sorrows. Meeting me at the Jaffa Gate he took me on a different route:

**RR**    I'm at the start of the Via Dolorosa, the Way of Sorrows, the route that Jesus took to Golgotha, but it's not the traditional route which most pilgrims follow. One of the people who thinks this is the actual Way of the Cross is Father Jerome Murphy O'Connor and he's with me now. Good morning, Father.

**JM**    Good morning.

**RR**    And Happy Easter to you.

**JM**    Thank you very much.

**RR**    Where exactly are we?

**JM**    We're just inside the Jaffa Gate, outside what is today the Citadel, which was the palace of Herod at the time of Jesus. That is why I think it is the historical Via Dolorosa because that's where Pilate would have been, and that's where the judgment of Jesus would have taken place.

**RR**    So take me down and tell me why you think the rest of this way is the real Dolorosa.

**JM**    Because slightly to our left behind these buildings would have been the city wall, the first wall of the city, that is the first north wall.

**RR**    Yes.

**JM**    And outside that was empty land and quarries and just inside it was a street leading to a city gate. Jesus would have been trying to get through a crowd jamming the streets with a big beam strung to his shoulders which meant he couldn't just walk forward – he would have had to shuffle sideways.

**RR**    Yes, but along this way we have none of the official stations.

**JM**    No, because the Via Dolorosa was really only fixed about the fourteenth or fifteenth century, when European pilgrims who experienced the stations of the Cross in Europe came back and said, 'Where are all the places here?' So these were instituted on the basis of European pilgrim pressure. But now, you see, we've turned to the north, we've come through the city gates.

**RR**    So we're out of the Gate.

**JM**    We're out of the Gate now. This would have been a quarry, because they found it here under this big church in front of us, the Lutheran Church, and they found it underneath the Holy Sepulchre. And Golgotha was in fact, a protuberance, of very poor stone left sticking out of one side of the quarry. On the other side of the quarry were tombs.

**RR**    Yes.

**JM**    And in between, when the quarry was abandoned about 100 BC, someone put in a layer of arable earth in which olive and carob trees were planted. And all this has been found by Father Korbel. And so it was in fact the garden, and they chose this

*36*

tomb because it was close, we are told. The Holy Sepulchre now is just ahead of us, behind that building.

To experience the Greek Orthodox Easter was a privilege. On both occasions it happened while I was sailing in the Mediterranean on the cruise ship the *Orpheus*. Memories of Easter in Nauplion are the sharpest. As I hoped to attend the Easter Eve midnight service and comment upon it I thought it was wise that I should find out a little of what was to happen. Hilary Mayo arranged for me to meet one of the local priests with an interpreter who would be able to give me the background to the service I was due to witness that evening. He explained to me that I would need to be early as the church would get very full. Fortunately, I took this advice. The church was packed. The rest of what happened bore little resemblance to what had been explained to me.

I had been told that just before midnight the lights in the church would go out and from a single flame behind the iconostasis, which is never extinguished, a candle would be lit. This candle would be brought to the congregation who, in turn, would light their candles which they would keep alight until they got home. Then with the smoke from the candle they would make the sign of the Cross on their home to act as a sign of blessing. At the hour of midnight the priest would process into the square outside the church, mount a rostrum, read the East Gospel and proclaim *Christos Anesti* – Christ is risen, to which the reply is *Alithos Anesti* – He is risen indeed. This would be the sign for firecrackers and general mayhem to begin.

What I actually witnessed was nowhere nearly so well ordered. At about quarter to midnight the lights in the church went out but there was far more than one flame flickering behind the iconostasis and as soon as the servers appeared with the lighting candles, many in the congregation rushed forward to light theirs. I have never been exposed to such a fire hazard. The mob, which is what the congregation had become by now, made their way out into the square. The priest, accompanied by servers and an icon, made his way to the dais in the square. His declaration that Christ had risen showed little sense of timing, taking place several minutes before midnight. After official greetings had been exchanged between priest and civic dignitaries the firecrackers did explode and the mayhem did begin. What made me rather sad was that few of the worshippers returned to the church for the rest of the service, which I believe still had more than an hour to go. I have to confess that I didn't stay. Having recorded my piece I returned to be honoured with an invitation from the captain of the *Orpheus* to join him, his family, and his crew for their Easter celebrations which consisted, amongst other things, of eating lamb and cracking eggs – hard boiled.

When the Western and Greek Orthodox Easter coincide all households traditionally dye eggs red in preparation for Easter Eve. They are the symbol of life and before starting to eat their Easter meal all the members of the family would clink the red eggs and while clinking them it was also a tradition to say *Christos Anesti*. The egg clinking ceremony that I experienced resembled more of a conker contest than something religious and deeply symbolic.

At all Christian festivals food and drink have always featured prominently and so they did on our programmes. Normally I would visit a home where food was being prepared. Kind families in America, Israel, Lapland, Austria and Greece were only too ready to welcome me into their homes to sample the various culinary delights. It was always good to share in the life of the people of the country I was visiting and I have to admit that many people seemed much more aware of the meaning of their traditions than I think people in parts of Britain are.

# RENDER UNTO CAESAR

Despite the fact that twenty-four bishops have seats in the House of Lords there is a strong feeling in Britain that politics and religion don't, or at least shouldn't, mix.

Most of the interviews of politicians took place either in the MP's home or in the Houses of Parliament. Few came to the studio. Interviewing MPs is not easy. Some are so well trained, and all are extremely experienced at answering questions, that it is not always easy to create and sustain an ordinary conversation. However, this was not difficult with Tony Benn, especially when I suggested that he was a rebel:

**RR**    Tony, you *are* a bit of a rebel, aren't you?

**TB**    No, I don't think so. I try to represent adequately the people who elect me, and I come from a tradition – you see, there's not just one tradition against which people rebel, that's one of the great illusions. There's only one correct position and everybody else is hard Left or extremist or whatever. There are two traditions in Britain, and they both have a very ancient history. One is of authority where you do what you're told, and the other is that everybody, every man and woman is a brother and sister and have an obligation to each other, and I mean I suppose I could argue that those who are always trying to get us under control are the rebels against the obligations of common fellowship. So that I think when you use the word 'rebel' you are establishing your own position and then judging me in reference to where you're standing, and I don't take that view at all.

**RR**    But you find authority, in some way, difficult to cope with?

**TB**    Well, I think the question is, where does the authority come from? I mean, I ask, when I see somebody with power – I always ask four or five questions: 'Where did you get your power from?', 'In whose interest do you exercise it?', 'To whom are you accountable?' and 'How can we get rid of you?'. Now until you ask those questions, whether it's multi-nationals or Rupert Murdoch, whether it's the Civil Service or the military, whether it's politicians or whoever it is, till you ask those questions, you don't understand your own position in the hierarchy, and God bless the squire and his relations and keep us in our proper stations, which is the old Victorian idea that there was a class structure with a King and Queen at the top and the peasant outside, and the peasant did what he was told, and that is the cause of an awful lot of suffering and injustice in the world, which is still very, very evident, even in a rich country like our own.

Paul Boateng, the MP for Brent North, was extremely easy to talk with. He is a Methodist lay preacher and for him, politics and faith go hand in hand. Although he does not wish to be known as a black politician his colour obviously gives him insights which are not so readily available to white politicians:

**RR**    Do you think in any way it's a special calling to be an MP and you also happen to be black? Does this produce tensions for you?

**PB**    It is a special calling in the sense that it brings with it a special responsibility, but foremost amongst those responsibilities is not to allow yourself to be typecast, stereotyped, you know, to be seen as a sort of silhouette, or a one-dimensional black cardboard cut-out, pulled on and off stage as a race agenda determines. Yes, I'm black and I glory in my African culture and tradition, just as I do in my mother's Scottish and British one. But I don't allow it – I don't get sort of trapped in the castle of my skin. It's a part of my life and it brings special responsibilities to make a success of a multi-racial democracy, but I want to be and am a fully rounded political personality with views and opinions on a wide range of topics, and not to be seen solely as, you know, a race spokesperson.

Many politicians find themselves debating moral issues, like capital punishment and abortion. On these issues the Party Whip is generally removed and conscience is allowed full part. But this does not protect politicians from pressure groups. On subjects like these people have strong feelings and do their utmost to make sure that their voices are heard and their influence exerted. David Alton, being a committed Roman Catholic, voiced strong views about abortion:

**RR**    Were you hurt terribly when your Bill was talked out – the abortion Bill?

**DA**    Well, I wasn't naive about it. It was the fifteenth attempt at pro-life legislation. I was very glad that it had got as far as it did, after all, no Bill had got further, no pro-life Bill had had so much support – 296 MPs had voted for it. It was never defeated on a single vote, and it was purely as a result of chicanery and trickery that finally our opponents managed to prevent it from making further progress, and I think that it heightened the debate – it ensured that people looked at the issues, and if this business is about changing attitudes and softening hearts, then I think the Bill has played its part. But obviously I want to see legislative change. It took

|    | the anti-slavery movement forty years and it may take pro-life forty years as well. |
|----|----|
| RR | Do you see it on the same level as anti-slavery? |
| DA | I think it's actually worse. You are destroying an unborn child, you are destroying life, and I think that we will all ultimately be answerable for that. And when you think about the barbaric practices allowed in this country where a baby as late as seven months into pregnancy can be ripped from its mother's womb, and can be broken into pieces; when babies can be removed using the prostaglandin process and struggle for hours on end for life, and then are placed in black sacks and incinerated. When you look at what we allow in this country under British law, you can see that it's even more barbaric and even less civilised than what we allowed during the Slave Trade. |
| RR | What about the opponents of the Bill, who felt, David, that you were imposing your particular values on the rest of the people and denying women their freedom? |
| DA | If I hadn't been able to get a majority of MPs to vote for what I believed was to be right, and to vote for the virtues of the Bill, then the Bill would not have made the progress that it did, and it's not a question of what I believe, it's a question of what Parliament believes. We have an upper time limit for abortions which has been in effect really since 1929 when the Infant Life Preservation Act was passed, which set a limit then of twenty-eight weeks, seven months into pregnancy. I think it's perfectly legitimate for any Member of Parliament to challenge the law when you think it's wrong. When people say it's their right to choose, they don't take any account of another person's right to life. It's never our right to choose to take somebody else's life – the right to life must *always* be paramount. |

\*

Actually we had to interview David twice. The first recording was due to be transmitted when the offer of someone we could not refuse was put on our plate and David's interview had to be shelved because when we came to transmit it, we realised that it had passed its sell-by date – circumstances had changed. In the meantime David had married so his circumstances had also changed, yet he very kindly agreed to re-do it. Not everyone would have been so obliging.

All the politicians I interviewed had a great love for the Houses of Parliament. Despite my criticism, which is the criticism of many, that they behave like a lot of argumentative children, they defend the House to the hilt.

The person responsible for keeping not just a Party in order, but the whole House of Commons, is the Speaker. Talking to a former Speaker, Lord Tonypandy, was always a delight, especially when he was talking about his roots:

**RR** What does the Rhondda mean to you?

**LT** Well, it's home, and there is no place like home. How true that is, the older you get, the more you realise it. When I go back there, I remind myself that my mother and father were born there, and my brothers and sisters. I wasn't – I was born in Port Talbot, because they had moved away, looking for work. I was back there before I was one year old, so my life has been in the Rhondda Valley.

**RR** You've always been so proud of your roots, though, haven't you, George? I mean, there's the miners' lamp on your coat of arms and the open Bible.

**LT** Yes, and the daffodil and the leek, because we can't make up our mind which is our emblem, but I wear both. However, we are very clannish in those valleys and when I was growing up I could tell the difference in accent from the Rhondda Valley, the Merthyr Valley and the Aberdare, and certainly the Monmouthshire Valleys – very different. Someone from outside Wales would think we all speak alike, but there are nuances and every valley has a deep cultural background.

RR    What effect do you think the valleys have had on your life? Or particularly the Rhondda?

LT    Oh well, you see, I happen to believe that every one of us is in part a creature of his environment, and in part uniquely himself, thanks to God's creation. Well, looking back from this great height of eighty years, I would still rather be born in a miner's cottage than in a Duke's palace.

Obviously, life as a politician these days is far from tranquil. Most of them find relaxation with their families and friends, but one senior politician whom I interviewed got tremendous pleasure out of what, for him, was a very important hobby. Edward Heath finds great enjoyment in his music making:

RR    How did you get your love of music?

EH    Well, I've had it for a very long time because I started learning the piano when I was seven. I think that came about because I had an aunt who was a very good pianist and I used to enjoy so much listening to her playing that I finally persuaded my parents to allow me to learn, and a teacher from the village taught me. Well, then I went on as a chorister in the parish church, and my voice broke so I then started to learn the organ. I didn't start conducting until I was fifteen and then when I went up to Oxford I became organ scholar of my college, looked after all the music in chapel, and also the music for the group which gave concerts every alternate Sunday evening. It was in fact the oldest musical society in Oxford and had a tremendous record of distinguished musicians and artists who appeared before it.

RR    What is an organ scholar expected to do at Oxford?

EH    It does vary to a certain extent from college to college, but I suppose the general phrase is the one

I use – that he is responsible for all the music in the college chapel. As far as I was concerned it meant an early morning service every weekday, which is why I have never been able to get up early since, and service on Sunday in chapel. We didn't have a permanent choir from the point of view of having a boys' choir or men's choir, and so on but we did have a number of members of the college who really formed the basis of the congregational singing in the chapel.

**RR**    With that sort of background did you ever think of becoming a professional musician?

**EH**    Well, yes. When I left Oxford it was in the summer of 1939 and I talked to the then professor of music at Oxford about this, Sir Hugh Allen – a most distinguished musician, rather an irascible character, but he said, 'Well, you've been President of the Union and you've studied politics and economics and all those horrible things, and you're a law scholar at Gray's Inn, so you could go and make a lot of money as a lawyer and then become a politician, or alternatively you could become a musician. And if you're going to be a musician, then you must be a conductor.' He also added that if you are going to be a great conductor you must be prepared to be as unpleasant as some of those are.

If you are interviewing members of the Commons you mustn't forget those who sit in the Upper House, the House of Lords. I had the privilege to interview two Lords, both connected with the law and both very active in the Lords. They were the former Lord Chancellor, Lord Hailsham, and that highly idiosyncratic judge, Lord Denning.

Lord Hailsham I had met before at Cumberland Lodge in Windsor Great Park. Lord Denning I had spoken to once as he sat on a seat waiting for his train on Waterloo station. Both their Lordships had kindly invited me to their homes for the interviews. Lord Hailsham in Wimbledon and Lord Denning in Hampshire. With Lord Hailsham I talked about his days as a boy at Eton but this was only a preliminary to hearing his views on many subjects including the family:

**RR**    How do you feel about the importance of the family?

**LH**    Well, I think it is of course the brick out of which society is built. No family – no stable society. I think it's fundamental to the existence of a stable society.

**RR**    Do you think the family is being undermined at the moment?

**LH**    I think it has been undermined, because of the failure to keep to the official doctrine of the Christian Church, that is to say, no sex outside marriage, outside marriage it's a sin. Also because of the habit which has now become socially respectable of what is called 'shacking up' and the apparently open action of prominent people in committing adultery.

**RR**    Why do you think that this has been allowed to happen?

**LH**    I think because people have lost their religious faith.

**RR**    You put quite a heavy emphasis on to sin. Do you think the Church teaches us enough these days?

**LH**    Well, I think that the old way of teaching it – about hell-fire – is probably not a very good thing, but I think that the Church ought to teach that the deprivation of God, whether it's in this life or in any future life, is the ultimate disaster which can overtake a man, and of course sin does cut you off from God.

Lord Denning fitted very comfortably into his surroundings in the beautiful countryside of Hampshire. He was more than pleased to still be in the county of his birth and his accent was as rural as ever. When I interviewed him he had recently celebrated his ninetieth birthday but he was as vital as ever. The next day a television company would call to record yet another interview. Amongst his birthday presents was a large-print edition of the Bible, Authorised Version of course.

I had heard that Lord Denning once found himself on the wrong side of the law – he pulled the communication cord on a train:

RR     You have done something that I've always wanted to do and never done, and that's pulled the communication cord on a train. Are you a man without fear?

LD     How did you find out?

RR     I have a note that tells me that.

LD     You have? It was when I was a very young barrister with almost my first brief. It was in a county court – I think down Greenwich way, and I got on the train and, blow, it didn't stop at Greenwich, and I felt I had to do my brief. I pulled the communication cord. Only time I did it and I managed – there weren't any taxis – I managed to get to the court, and to do my case. Then I had letters afterward, if you please, from the railway company wanting to fine me for pulling the cord . . .

RR     And did they?

LD     No, I wrote a good letter in answer. I said it was their fault for putting me on the wrong train.

RR     But you've always been a bit of a rebel. Does this worry you at all?

LD     Oh, I'm not a rebel, I'm just getting my own way.

RR     Over what sort of subjects?

LD     Well, in a way I fight for what I think is right and just. Indeed, I told a little story the other day – I'm the president of the Basingstoke Male Voice Choir and they gave a party for me, and talking to that choir I said, 'When I was a boy, my five brothers all sang in our church choir. The vicar gave me a test and I chose the hymn, "Fight the good fight". He turned me down most unjustly, and I've been fighting for justice ever since.'

RR     And do you feel that you've succeeded, or do you think the weight of things is against you?

**LD**    Oh, I've succeeded sometimes, but there's an awful lot of weight against it. Oh, no, no, in the Court of Appeal, you know, I often found myself in a minority of one and I always used to say, 'When I was a judge of first instance sitting alone, I *could* and *did* do justice.' In the Court of Appeal of three, I found the chances of doing justice were two to one against, because I would be dissenting.

Also in the House of Lords, but this time from the Chilterns, comes another of my interviewees, Lord Miles, better known as Bernard Miles the actor and founding father of the City of London's only theatre, the Mermaid. He had recently made a recording called 'God's Brainwave' which retold the stories of Jesus in dialect. Bernard was born into a non-conformist family and as a child had loved hearing his grandfather reading him Bible stories in the language of his native heath. He knew the stories were mostly about working-class people and their occupations and so he set about retelling the stories of Jesus as he remembered his grandfather telling them in his Hertfordshire speech. During the interview I discussed with him how he came to record 'God's Brainwave'. But he really told me why he was a Christian:

**RR**    Bernard, how did you come to record 'God's Brainwave'?

**BM**    Well, I was brought up a Christian. My mother was a Wesleyan – I think Methodist, or whatever they call themselves, and because the Baptist chapel was nearer than the Wesleyan when I came to be four and a half I was packed off there. And I soaked in Christianity. I don't know if I was born to be a Christian – I mean there have been times when I have resisted it, but I think I'm a born, sort of born Christian.

It wasn't only British politicians who appeared on the programme; I was amazed at the very easy access I was able to have to Dr Garrett FitzGerald, who was at that time the

Taoiseach of Ireland. Even though it was his wife's birthday he very kindly came into his office on a Saturday morning to record an interview. I was always slightly overawed meeting people in such positions as Dr FitzGerald but he couldn't have been easier to talk to, though I did have to listen carefully to make sure that I understood everything he said in that gentle Irish accent:

**RR**    Wasn't your parents' a mixed marriage – wasn't your mother from the North and your father from the South?

**GF**    Yes, my mother was a northern Presbyterian who didn't become a Catholic until quite late in life, after over thirty years in married life.

**RR**    Did she mind making the change?

**GF**    No, no, the change was her choice – my father never pestered her at all, and she came to the decision over a long period of time. She in fact didn't practise as a Presbyterian and did carry the responsibility of our religious upbringing – it was she who taught us our religion, as she had promised to do on marriage, and in the process of teaching us our religion, she eventually came to the conclusion that Catholicism, although she had difficulties with aspects of it, was the religion that she preferred to end her life in.

**RR**    She was obviously a very disciplined lady to be prepared as a Protestant to bring up her children as Catholics . . . that's a very positive way of thinking.

**GF**    Well, she had promised to do so, and she was a Presbyterian, with a very strong Presbyterian sense of duty and obligation when a promise had been made.

**RR**    Did she take you to Mass?

**GF**    Oh yes, oh yes.

**RR**    But would you find it odd that she wouldn't go up to receive the sacrament?

**GF**    Well, what actually happened was that I didn't notice this, because I was quite small, until one day

I was sitting on the floor in front of her when I made a disparaging remark about a Protestant – then our deputy Prime Minister – I mean, disparaging about his religion. I cannot conceive where, at the age of five, I had apparently acquired this element of bigotry. My mother just looked down at me and said, 'But you do know I'm a Protestant too, dear, don't you?' which I didn't until that moment. But with that revelation to me, I have endeavoured to be ecumenical ever since.

The American political scene meant little to me. We tried to interview both Ronald Reagan and Jimmy Carter but sadly failed. However, we did interview a person who aspired to the White House and who knew it quite well. I caught up with Presidential Candidate, and former Christian minister, Pat Robertson in his hotel in California where he was recording his television show. My producer on this occasion was Hilary Mayo, who for some reason spent most of the time on the floor trying to balance the recording equipment. Caught up with these technicalities, at one stage she didn't realise that although the interview was still progressing we had actually run out of recording tape! There was an added distraction. From her vantage point on the floor she noticed that although Pat Robertson was wearing a smartly tailored pin-stripe suit, on his feet were cowboy boots. Pat saw a clash between his faith and his politics:

RR    How essential did you feel it was to resign your actual orders, of being a minister in your particular Church?

PR    We have a strong tradition in the United States of separation of Church and State, and I didn't want to be the one to blur the distinction between a man who holds a very honoured political post or a man who holds an equally honoured post as a member of the ordained clergy. So I thought I wanted to make a statement when I became an official candidate that I was doing it as a layman, not as a clergyman.

**RR**    Now did you have the backing of your Church for that?

**PR**    Yes, I conferred with three past presidents of my denomination, the Southern Baptists are the largest Protestant denomination in America, I consulted with these men, told them what I had in mind, and on their advice, I resigned from the local congregation where I had been ordained.

**RR**    Would you think of taking up your ministry again?

**PR**    Well, in a sense a person who is ordained by God can't resign it, it's a lifetime's commitment, and God's ordination has been on me for a number of years in continuance, so I am still in the ministry of the Lord in a very strong way. But I am not particularly interested in being ordained again as a clergyman.

**RR**    You may have heard, the British public gets slightly panicky about clergymen mixing religion and politics. Do you find any worry in that field at all?

**PR**    There's a great deal of feeling that way. The reason is, it's understandable – first of all, people admire clergymen, they're men of God and their function is to lead people to God, to Jesus, to Salvation, not to get involved in what most people consider is dirty business. The second thing – many people also feel that clergymen are there to make them live better. They don't want their Prime Minister or President to tell them how to live – they think that's a job that's outside the sphere of government. So those two reasons account for a great deal of the antipathy against clergy in politics.

One person well acquainted with the inside of the White House was Charles Colson. He had spent some time in prison for his part in the Watergate scandal:

**RR**    I'm talking to Charles Colson about his very real and life commitment to Christ and his conversion which led him to set up Prison Fellowship Ministries. How did that come about, Charles?

CC  Well, it really grew out of my own experiences, Roger, when I was in prison. I thought I would get out of prison and forget it and put it behind me, which is really what everyone who's been in prison wants to do.

RR  And you had the support of your family all the way through?

CC  Oh yes. They were wonderful. Though it was a shock to my wife who was very traditional in her religious upbringing and suddenly I come home with friends, praying in the living room. But it drew us very much closer together and I discovered something in prison – I discovered several things in prison – I really can look back now gratefully over my prison experiences, much as Alexander Solzhenitsyn writes about his experiences in prison: 'Bless you prison, bless you for being in my life, for there lying on the rotting prison straw I came to realise that the object of life is not prosperity as we are made to believe, but the maturing of the soul.' Ten years in prison. I learned that same lesson in prison but I also saw the futility of prisons to change people's lives. And I know you have had this problem in Britain as we have had in the United States.

RR  Oh absolutely. Yes.

CC  The prison – you put people in these cages and expect them to be transformed. They're transformed, but in a way that is counter-productive.

RR  They're becoming universities of crime.

CC  Exactly. And in the United States the statistics are very similar to England – our statistics are 75 per cent of the people commit new crimes when they get out. I can remember talking to some of your officials in the Home Office a couple of years ago, and they told me that the statistics in the United Kingdom were almost exactly the same. And so it's an appalling waste of humanity and a tremendous waste of taxpayers' money.

**RR** So are you saying that there are some people in prison who shouldn't be there?

**CC** Well, yes. And that's something we do get into in our ministry, which is advocating community service projects, something you have experimented with and used very effectively in Britain, and something we are using now in the United States. We make a big mistake in the prisons in Western societies today when we put people in prison and expect that they are going to be rehabilitated, and instead – and we put them there at enormous cost – instead they should be back out on the street working, paying back their victims and doing something redemptive in their own lives. And so we do advocate that. But our ministry grew, not as a reform movement – that is something that has grown out of it – our ministry began really as proclaiming the Gospel, as going into the prisons, setting up discipleship programmes. Today, in America, we are in almost six hundred prisons with twenty-five thousand volunteers.

An American politician I found fascinating to interview was the Mayor of Atlanta, Georgia, Andrew Young. He is well known to British listeners because of his time with the United Nations. It was, however, his reflections on modern-day Atlanta, especially the situation regarding race relations, that I wanted to hear:

**RR** Now the symbol of Atlanta is the Phoenix, risen from the ashes. Do you see Atlanta as a city of hope, on this Easter Day?

**AY** Well, I certainly do and that comes out of our being almost burned to the ground by General Sherman in our civil war, and I think we responded very much like London responded from the Blitz. At times like that people pull together and it really does bring out the best in people.

**RR** You worked very closely with Dr Martin Luther King, so you knew his mind. Do you think he would be proud of the way things are going in Atlanta at the moment?

**AY** I think he'd be proud, I think he'd be surprised that they're going as well as they are, but I think he'd still be very much upset by some of our problems.

**RR** What would you say were the things that were going well?

**AY** Well, we have probably created more jobs in the last five years, than the whole of Europe, some 670,000 jobs, more than fifty billion dollars in new investment, and that economic growth and vitality has been shared, black and white alike. I think he'd also be proud of the fact that we are becoming a truly international city. Human rights was never a major part of the American vocabulary and certainly not a part of our politics until Jimmy Carter, our Georgia Governor, became President of the United States. And suddenly – in a way it's the Martin Luther King agenda – it became a global agenda and everybody now is very conscious of the necessity for protecting the human rights of all our citizens.

**RR** Where would you see the tears in Martin Luther King's eyes, now?

**AY** When he faced the homeless. In spite of our growth and development, there's been a complete abandonment by the Federal Government of low and moderate income housing, and interest rates have been so high that housing just is not affordable. So we, in a city like this, in spite of all of our success, and in spite of the jobs, have mainly six to ten thousand people who are homeless on our streets. We have fifty-one churches that open their doors each night to give people shelter for the night and an evening meal, and the city operates three or four major centres that are there to make sure that nobody has to sleep on the streets.

**RR** Now before you became Mayor and were so involved in politics, you were in fact a Christian minister. Do you think the Churches played a good part in the civil rights movement?

**AY** Churches have played a very good part in the civil rights movement and an even better part in the movement to deal with the problems of poverty and homelessness. The Churches have really been a moral leader on this.

**RR** Do you think the Gospel, particularly this Easter Day, is preached well by the Churches here in Atlanta?

**AY** Well, it is and it isn't. I think we preach the Gospel of Easter which is a Gospel of hope and a Gospel of triumph, which I agree with, but we like to slide over the Gospel of Good Friday, and after all there can't be resurrections without crucifixions, and I think one of the reasons for the effectiveness of Martin Luther King's legacy is there was, in fact, a giving of his life for the things that he believed in and we have seen a social and political resurrection as a result of it. But, no Cross, no crown, and many people would like to have the crown of glory, but they don't want to go through the trial and the tribulation, or even a little bit of suffering.

On the whole, the politicians I interviewed saw no objections to the Church being involved in politics. After all, politics and religion are both about a way of life and so are bound to affect one another. But I have been glad to steer clear of party political in-fighting. The only loser would have been me.

# THE OTHER SIDE

Image making has become big business, not only for products but also for humans. Once that image has been established and accepted by the public then everything possible is done to preserve it. The guests on *Good Morning Sunday* had the opportunity, because of the relaxed non-controversial nature of the interviews, to be themselves rather than the image usually projected.

Shirley Bassey, speaking about the death of her mother and her daughter, showed another side of the flamboyant singer:

RR     What did your mother mean to you?

SB     Oh, everything. I mean, when she died I felt that a light went off somewhere in my life, because that was my contact.

RR     You relied on her.

SB     Yeah, and then she was suddenly gone and I thought, 'Now, who do I turn to?' and as grown-up as I was and as old as I was . . .

RR     So how did you cope with that loneliness?

SB     Very difficult. It was a very difficult period for me. I stopped singing for all of six months – I really didn't care. Like when I lost my daughter – the same thing. For my daughter I stopped a whole year. I mean, I did not really want to . . .

RR     That must have been a terrible shock when she died, in the Avon.

SB    It was awful. I mean to lose a daughter is something. Children should bury their parents, you know, and not the other way around. I buried my mother but that was another kind of shock. This woman gave birth to me, and she was my life-line.

RR    But how did you then cope with the grief, because you still had to perform? The work had to go on, didn't it?

SB    I just gave in. I just did not cope. I mean, I was a wreck.

RR    Were there any times when you thought I'll pack this all in . . .

SB    Yes, of course.

RR    . . . and I'll just go away to Switzerland and that's the end of it?

SB    Yes, and what got me back on the road was the fact that one day a voice said to me, 'Mother wouldn't . . .', you know it was my voice, 'she wouldn't like you to give up', because my mother was my greatest fan.

RR    Did it ever make you then think about God at all, or were you just angry with God that this had happened?

SB    No, I was not angry with God.

RR    You weren't?

SB    No. No, I was not angry with God. My mother was eighty but she was in perfect health, and – she just went like that, and it was the shock. If she'd been ill for any length of time, one can sort of say, 'Well, she's out of pain' and you could deal with it, but she was so healthy, and last time I saw her she was laughing.

RR    But you felt that you had to cope with this on your own, you didn't feel that you could turn to God, or could turn to religion in any way at all?

SB    I couldn't even turn to my sisters. It was something that I had to do all by myself.

\*

It was also a revelation to me to hear about her early years in the chamberpot-making factory:

RR    Is this when you were packing lavatory pans?

SB    Well, I was packing all household pans and sometimes lavatory pots, I mean the under-the-bed pots . . .

RR    The guzunders?

SB    . . . the guzunders came into it. I used to leave notes in those 'cos they were going around the world, you know, and they actually did get letters back.

RR    Did you?

SB    Yes, I used to leave my name and address, and say 'Please write to me. I'm a lonely little girl in this factory' and funny little things like that.

RR    But then you were singing in the evenings, weren't you?

SB    I used to go into competitions.

RR    Did you?

SB    Yes, and it's true what they say – never play opposite children and animals. I always came second. It was always an animal that won, or a child younger than me, and I was only a kid myself.

Someone whose work I had seen at fairly close range over a number of years was that of the Archbishop of Canterbury, Robert Runcie. When I interviewed him for Remembrance Sunday I was interested to hear his reaction to having been a fighting soldier:

RR    What memories have you got of the last world war?

AC    I've got memories of comradeship and I've got memories of extreme fright. I've got memories that are amusing, poignant. I think one of the most dramatic memories is in the battle after we'd crossed the Rhine and I was feeling somewhat triumphant because we had managed to man-oeuvre ourselves into a position and been able to hit a German tank which was holding up our advance. And after the battle was over, I walked over to the tank and was feeling pretty invigorated, things were quiet, and climbed up on to it, and I saw the four dead people – Germans – in the tank, and I felt slightly – not slightly – I felt very sick. And there flashed across one's mind, in the way that is imprinted on your memory for ever, how will this news be received at home, and these people are just like the people from the tank I've just left across the hill.

RR    Now of course you weren't ordained at this time, were you?

AC    Oh no. Far from it.

RR    Were you ever frightened yourself?

AC    Often. I think that people who say they are not frightened in war have forgotten.

RR    What do you think you have learnt from the war yourself?

AC    Well, I must say all sorts of good things. I learnt a lot about toleration. You can't live with a small group of people, of very different backgrounds and not learn something and value people that you would perhaps never meet or you might easily dismiss because they didn't do the kind of things you did. I, yes, learnt that it's not always the people who speak loudest who, when the chips are down, act most impressively. I suppose that has made me very cautious about judging people, because I did make some of the firmest friends that have been lifelong for me and have always been quick to rally round if they think I'm going through a hard time – they're not necessarily the most religious among my friends. But war itself is always a failure. People are infected by the violence of war, and in a world where we're so inter-dependent the victor suffers some corruption as much as the one defeated. But that's not to say that within war there are not values which we have often forgotten, and there's a certain nobility of the human spirit which you can't deny – I can't deny – it's a great mystery and a great puzzle, which you don't always find in days when people are self-indulgent and self-centred.

On another occasion I was pleased to find that he had time to relax; I thought the place where he did his relaxing was very wise indeed because all he had to do was nip across the road. Opposite Lambeth Palace in London is the famous St Thomas's Hospital, dedicated to one of the Archbishop's troublesome predecessors, Thomas à Becket. In this hospital is a swimming pool which the staff may use and now and again members of the medical profession were surprised to see the figure of one of the nation's leading churchmen, resplendent in his bathing costume, doing a few lengths.

A person with a very definite image in many people's eyes is the campaigner Mary Whitehouse. When I went to her home in Essex to interview her, she made us extremely welcome. I had met her before when she'd come to Eton to speak, an experience which I didn't think she'd enjoyed. In her own home she couldn't have been more relaxed as I interviewed her for the Mothering Sunday programme. Although Mary is a great fighter when it comes to the quality and content of what we watch and hear, there have been times when she has had to struggle hard within her own life:

**RR**    Motherhood hasn't been entirely easy for you. You had the terrible sadness of your twins dying.

**MW**    Yes.

**RR**    How did you cope with that?

**MW**    Well, I was told when I was six months pregnant that I was going to have twins. I was told at that time that they were likely to be very delicate and I was advised to have an abortion. Now that was something I could not accept and my husband couldn't accept. We felt that it was right to go through and on with the pregnancy and I did go just about full-term. The first one was born alive, but then died very shortly afterwards, and the second one was born dead. Now, circumstances then –

that's, what forty-five years ago – were very different in the care of mothers and babies, and I was left alone a great deal of the time. And I remember – oh, because this had happened, my friends absolutely poured flowers at me – my room was full of flowers. But my bridesmaid had sent me a little bunch of lilies of the valley, and I had this on my table, on my bedtable in front of me. And as I lay there, and I was just looking at those flowers, two of those little florets turned into babies' faces, and they were smiling, and they were happy faces. And, do you know, as I looked at them, looked at those flowers, I knew they were all right, I knew who they were with – the Lord was looking after them, and they were happy. And, do you know, it lifted all the sorrow and sadness and everything from me, and I have felt from that day and I still feel, when I think about it, I had five children, not three. And those two babies are still part of our family, so I don't regret it.

Botanist David Bellamy gave a certain 'greenness' to the *Good Morning Sunday* programme back in 1987. I have always enjoyed listening to him and watching him, partly because of the energy and effort one sees in all his performances. His enthusiasm comes across the minute you meet him and the arms go into perpetual motion the moment the green light goes on. He has managed to fulfil that extremely difficult task of making a technical subject available and understandable to a vast audience. People who would normally show little or no interest in the flora and fauna of a country are drawn to know more by David's presentation. He had his father to thank for his early interest. His father was a pharmacist who had an interest in plants with healing properties and now and again, to escape from the horrors of war, David would explore anywhere there was natural vegetation. Once the war was over David was taken to the seaside and this, for him, was a great adventure. So his love for all creatures and plants, great and small, wet and dry, began.

At the end of the programme, however, I saw another side of David which was new to me. We started talking about his family and his churchgoing habits, and what had started as a straightforward question developed into an animated discussion:

**DB**    The First Commandment in the Bible was to have dominion, and dominion to me is wise rule. It is reaping the benefit for the rest of the things – the five, ten million species with which we share this planet. Reaping the benefits through good husbandry, through wise rule – not smashing it up or sending it to the wall of extinction.

**RR**    Is this why you and your wife decided to adopt children, because you felt that you ought to be responsible as regards population control in this world?

**DB**    Well, no, we always said we would have two, and we would adopt two. I do spend more of my time sort of going round lecturing about population *concern* – I'd rather call it, than control – than anything else, because whatever conservation does, you know, if the world population isn't contained in some way then, you know, we are living in cloud cuckoo land. But this leads me up to my greatest problem, I think. I mean, I go to Church as often as I can when I am at home, and my wife and children go up and they take Communion, and the ones that aren't old enough go and take the blessing. Now I haven't been able to take Communion for a long, long time, and I don't know why. I try – every Sunday I sit there in the pew and I think, 'Well, this Sunday I'll go up and ask', and I can't . . .

**RR**    Why, what stops you?

**DB**    Because I don't think that I have worked hard enough to do what I feel I can do . . .

**RR**    Yes, but Communion isn't a reward.

**DB**    I know it isn't a reward but it is that final statement, you know.

**RR**    No, I don't think it can be a final statement, David.

I think it has got to be a continuing thing. It's the thing of being re-charged and going on, and setting new demands for yourself.

**DB**  But I – the last time I took Communion, I turned around from the altar, totally ashamed that I had done this thing, because it was such an imperfect world. We hadn't got to that point of even understanding the imperfections so that we can make it perfect.

**RR**  But in that Communion is the statement that we ought to be ashamed, that someone has had to give their lives for us, and it is the challenge then to go on and do better. I don't think you should look on Communion as being a reward. I think that it should be something that strengthens you to spur you on.

**DB**  I don't know that I would look upon it as a reward – I look upon it as an act of faith, and I don't know that I have that 100 per cent faith in the Christian Church at the moment, because it isn't putting its back behind the one problem which faces this world. We are seeing God's creation smashed to pieces, and I don't actually think that the Christian Church is doing very much about that. I hope one day I will be able to go back and say, 'Yes, I do understand the very point you are making' because it is pretty lonely sitting there in our tiny little church, seeing the family go up and take Communion, and know I can't.

Comments about attendance at Church reveal quite a lot about some of the guests which had previously lain hidden to the public eye and ear. For instance, weatherman Ian McCaskill told us what he got up to on his way to and from Communion:

**RR**  Now, when did you meet your wife, because this was travelling around the world somewhere, wasn't it?

**IMcC**   Well, this is one of those things that I don't think was any accident in the world. I wasn't going to meet her where she lived in the Pennines, and she applied for this job in Geneva at the same time as I applied for this job in Geneva, and we would have met there, that's – willy nilly. But inexplicably, we both didn't get through to the interview so then we both volunteered at the same time for service in Malta, the foreign legion I think it was in those days, and she went out to teach with the navy and I went out to do the weather with the air-force and there we met.

**RR**   Now she isn't a weather lady – there weren't the two of you in one house going in and coming out?

**IMcC**   Oh no. No, indeed no. But I think Somebody was determined I should meet this woman.

**RR**   That's lovely. And you've got two children, now.

**IMcC**   Oh, two daughters, and they are the apple of my eye. They're lovely. I shall miss them at Church this morning – they'll both be singing in the choir . . .

**RR**   Will they?

**IMcC**   . . . and that's one of my happiest moments in life, I think, when you're waiting to take Communion and just leaning over and shocking the old ladies in the choir by ruffling the girls' hair as they sing away!

**RR**   That's very nice because that joins you with your family as you go for Communion.

**IMcC**   I think so. I know it's a bit . . .

**RR**   But this isn't Church of Scotland down here, is it?

**IMcC**   Ah, ah, no. It's – it's Church of England. I did sort of scout about looking for the local Church of Scotland, but I soon found out that the Church of England was just the same – they just talked a bit funny.

The thought of actress Kathy Staff singing her heart out in her Church choir brought a new image to light. I forgot to ask her whether the choir robes that she wore covered her wrinkled stockings but it was good to hear that, despite her heavy schedule recording such programmes as *The Last of the Summer Wine*, she still found the time to sing the praises of the Lord!

**RR**    Were you a good choirgirl? I mean, were you good at practice and things like that?

**KS**    Well, yes, when I was younger. But then of course when the work came up, which took me away, I wasn't able to go to the practices as much as I used to.

**RR**    Were there fears about you becoming an actress? Did your parents think, 'Oh, she's wandering from the straight and narrow'?

**KS**    I don't think so. My mother, who had a wonderful voice, she should have been an opera singer, really – she had a fantastic voice – she always wanted me to be an opera singer because she couldn't. She had me trained as a singer, but I chose the dramatic side rather. But I got every encouragement really, which was wonderful because nobody else in the family ever went on stage.

Someone who could not always make it to Church was ace detective Hercule Poirot, played by actor David Suchet. On such Sundays, however, he made sure that there was worship in the home:

**RR**    Aren't there times actually when you have quiet times with the children, which they rather like?

**DS**    Yes.

**RR**    And may we know what happens then?

**DS**    Well, that actually is perhaps my greatest joy, to be with them in this journey towards Christ, and into Christ. I find that when I say to the children, 'Look, we're not going to Church today, we're going to have a quiet time' they actually say 'Hooray!', which is lovely for Dad, really. I don't know whether I'm doing the best thing for the Church but it's lovely for Dad.

**RR**    Yes.

**DS**    And we do, we read together, read the modern version, sometimes the New International, sometimes the Good News, and we discuss what's written from their point of view. And they talk about their week at school and what they have been doing and we sing, and we dance, and then Mummy and Daddy sometimes act out the situations that we read about in the Bible, like the Good Samaritan.

**RR**    How superb.

**DS**    And they become part of it and we do a little play, because after all, I'm in the business . . .

**RR**    I should think they're getting the best Sunday School any child could possibly have.

**DS**    Well, it's fun and I enjoy it too. And you see, I don't know much about the Bible at all, I'm coming to it as anybody comes to it, and it's not an easy book.

**RR**    No it isn't.

**DS**    It's a very difficult book and let's face it, it's not easy but, by goodness, it is worth it. And once you're into it and you see the situations and the drama and the potential of what's in there, actually it's so good – there's so much fun in there as well. It's not all dour and holy, holy, holy – it's great. I've read some stories in the Bible that I would say play the greatest theatre in the world.

As I mentioned earlier, Malcolm and Kitty Muggeridge were guests that we had on the programme twice and on both occasions we went to their hideaway home in Sussex to interview them. Malcolm was certainly a person who in the past had a very definite image. With his skilled pen and sharp and witty tongue he made quite a name for himself as one of the most compelling broadcasters of his generation. He was also a rebel. Although when I met him he had lost none of his sparkle, he appeared far less the rebel. Kitty, I am sure, could take much of the credit for this new-found peace at the heart of Malcolm, and so as we talked, it was only right that we should reflect on the value of love:

RR    But let's recapture your thoughts on love. I
      know that you've got one of Shakespeare's Sonnets
      there . . .

MM    Yes.

RR    . . . which really sort of sums up your marriage.
      Malcolm, would you read it for us?

MM    I'd love to read it. It's a beautiful sonnet.
          Let me not to the marriage of true minds
          Admit impediments. Love is not love
          Which alters when it alteration finds;
          Or bends with the remover to remove:
          Oh, no! It is an ever-fixed mark,
          That looks on tempests, and is never shaken.
          It is the star to every wandering bark,
          Whose worth's unknown, although his height be
              taken.
          Love's not Time's fool, though rosy lips and
              cheeks
          Within his bending sickle's compass come;
          Love alters not with his brief hours and weeks,
          But bears it out even to the edge of doom.
          If this be error, and upon me proved,
          I never writ and no man ever loved.

It was Kitty who helped Malcolm deepen his faith, but the
roots had been there for some time:

RR    Does it ever worry you that you came to a deep
      faith rather late in life?

MM    Not really, not really, because it had been floating
      about in my mind for years before, when I was even
      at school. For instance, curious thing – I was going
      through all my books at home and I had found a
      Bible of which the pages had all sort of folded over,
      and I remembered that when I was in the senior
      classes at school I used to find a place in the Bible
      which related to what I wanted and put it – bend it
      over – and put it under my head when I went to
      sleep.

It was new-found faith that had transformed the life of another performer. Bobby Ball, along with his partner Tommy Cannon, had been bringing enjoyment to their fans for a great number of years. As private individuals I knew very little about them but when I was in Blackpool for a seaside special I was told some news which surprised and delighted me. I was walking back along one of Blackpool's piers with the singer Dana, having just seen and enjoyed the summer show she was in with Joe Longthorne and Roy Walker, talking about other people who were appearing in summer shows that year. She asked me whether I'd heard the news that Bobby Ball had become a Christian. Dana, who is a good friend of *Good Morning Sunday* and has also presented the programme, thought he would make a good guest but that we should wait until he was more established in his faith. We did wait; in fact we waited over a year until we tracked him down in a hotel in Farnborough in Hampshire. This was done with the help of Dave Berry, who was also associated with the Arts Centre Group. By this time Bobby was more than ready to talk:

**RR**   Bobby, a very significant thing has happened to you in the last, sort of eighteen months when you became a born-again Christian. How did that come about?

**BB**   It came about because I've always been searching, or never really totally satisfied. I'm not a material person, and I've never been really satisfied or – truly content. I've always searched for things, and I've been through Buddhism and I've been through every religion there is, really. And they could never give me the true answers really, you see. And then I've been on the road with Tommy for a long time, and, I've a lovely wife at home and I felt rather guilty.

**RR**   What – that you were missing out, or she was missing out, not being . . .

**BB**   Not the way I've treated her, and things I'd done. Maybe the way I'd treated her. And a friend of mine called Max Wigley, who's a minister in Bradford, he does the Bradford Alhambra Theatre . . .

**RR**    Oh, the chaplain there.

**BB**    The chaplain there, yeah. But I've known him for years and years, you see. We went there eighteen months ago for a season and he came in and I had started arguing with him about religion – not arguing, it was a discussion, you know – why do you always wear your dog-collar and, how do you know there's a God, and – the usual. Then I said, 'I feel guilty about my wife, you know. I'm not that nice a person, really.' I used to be very angry and – moods changing . . .

**RR**    What, through nerves?

**BB**    Yeah, through nerves. And then he said, 'Well, why don't you come and pray with me?' and I said, 'Oh, I can't be doing with that', you know, 'I've never been to Church in my life.' And for some reason, I went up to his house, ten-thirty it was, in the morning, and I went into his study with him, and he said, 'Why don't you pray then, and ask for forgiveness for what you've done wrong?' So I said to him, 'How do you know what I've done wrong?' He said, 'None of us are perfect, Bob. If you feel guilty and you want peace of mind, try it. You want Him in, don't you?' and I did. But I thought my life would have to change so drastically – it frightened me to death, 'cos I thought the step was so big. I got on my knees and prayed and I couldn't finish what I was saying 'cos I just started crying and I knew that Jesus was very real.

**RR**    And did you find a huge release in this?

**BB**    I found I was starting again. I knew what 'born-again' meant then. And I felt my life was just starting then.

Three guests have made life difficult for me: Sir Harry Secombe, Les Dawson and Ken Dodd. And that's not because they wouldn't answer questions, but because of the way they answered them. All three, in my estimation, are very funny men. Their humour permeates everything they do and once I start laughing there's no holding me. Sir Harry has quite a good laugh in his own right and when the two of us were at it, the recording engineer twiddled with knobs as fast as he could trying to reduce the pain-factor passing through his ears. The decibels must have risen so high that it destroyed the tapes because, sadly, I have been unable to find any recordings of my interviews with Sir Harry. I have three memories that have certainly remained.

It was a privilege to see Harry at work with one of the BBC orchestras. They obviously respected him and he them. If something did go wrong Harry would blow one of his Goon-type raspberries and they would start all over again. He was also kind enough to telephone me live on air on my last *Good Morning Sunday* broadcast, during my chat with Thora Hird. At one time I thought we would never get the next record on as the three of us were so enjoying one another's company. My third memory is in book form. When Harry published his *Highway Companion* he was kind enough to give me a copy, which he signed to his 'Arch-rival'.

Les Dawson I had met through a good friend, Ruth Madoc, when they were in pantomime together in Manchester. As always, Les, with the rest of the cast, had been packing them into the Palace Theatre, breaking all box office records. And despite the laughter that shook the building night after night life was not quite so buoyant in the dressing room. At the time Les's first wife was dying. The cast included that marvellous dance troupe the Roly Polys and along with Les's dresser, they were determined that at no time would he be left on his own when he was off stage. In such a cut-throat profession it was good to witness such quality of care. But as for religion, well, that was different:

RR     You're not a great lover of religion, are you?
LD     Not man-made religions, no.
RR     Why is that?
LD     Well, it's the interpretation that causes more trouble than ever. You see, to me, dogma, pure

dogma – man-made dogma is always open to misinterpretation anyway. I mean we build mammoth cathedrals and God knows what, when actually Christ himself preached on a hillside. And I can never quite understand – I can never correlate the two together. So I'm religious in myself and I bring the kids up to, you know, realise they're not the be-all and end-all, but I'm not religious in the man-made concept.

**RR**    So where do you see the sort of difference between faith and religion? I mean, you see religion as purely the organised thing, don't you?

**LD**    Hmm.

**RR**    Where do you see faith?

**LD**    Within everybody. Within us all – you carry it with you.

**RR**    In what sort of way?

**LD**    In your daily habits, in the way you live your life. I mean most people live a very good life in this world. I find I always have a strange feeling that the power of evil is a very real thing, I think. Partly the demise of the Church, the Christian Church, has been the fact that they have refuted the Devil. I think evil is with us, and very strong, but I don't think it's man-made evil.

**RR**    So you don't see evil as the sort of the horns and the hooves and the tail?

**LD**    No, not in that sense, no. It's subtle evil – it can be evil in somebody who is – who goes and sits in a church and prays for everything, holier than thou can be an evil. You see in the great scheme of things I don't believe that the way we interpret good and evil is the answer. I mean, a man might have led a life that seems by our standards desolate, but in the greater scheme of things, possibly not, because everybody's life is an experience – a singular experience.

**RR**    So how do you feel people should cope with evil?

**LD**    By trying to look at their own lives first – and then by putting others first. If you do that there is no two ways about it – you get more satisfaction out of life.

With most guests you have no worry whatsoever as to whether they will turn up or not. Agents or managers bring them, or cars are sent for them. With Ken Dodd it is a whole different ball game. He comes under his own steam but as to when he will come, that is anybody's guess. We had arranged to meet Ken at the BBC studios in Liverpool. Having travelled up from London that morning we prepared ourselves for what could have been a long wait. Despite the worst forebodings Ken arrived on time and with a tickling stick which he gave me as a present. I have always been a fan of Ken's, ever since I took my young nephew and niece to see him in pantomime in Coventry. Along with the Diddy Men he kept me (I'm not so sure about my nephew and niece) transfixed for three hours. To meet him was a privilege. He delighted me by asking me for my autograph so that he could give it to his cleaning lady – a fan of *Good Morning Sunday*.

The interview I did with Ken has been lost, but I was fortunate to find a tape of an interview he did with my predecessor, Paul McDowell, and was fascinated by his views on humour:

**PMcD**    How did you develop this sense of humour and this ability to look askance at everything and almost, you know, put the proverbial . . .

**KD**    Well, everybody has a sense of humour, that's such a God-given gift. You've been given this ability to see things a little differently and to pick out the whimsical bits and also to laugh. Laughter is a wonderful gift from heaven. There's a rainbow of laughter. I think, it's like a rainbow. And at the very, very top there's sheer joy. If you want to hear that you have to pass a school playground. When you pass a school playground you hear little children laughing for the sheer joy of being alive. They're not telling jokes, I don't think so anyway, they're all just running around laughing their heads off, just for the sheer joy of life. Then, as you

72

progress down the rainbow of laughter you get all the different kinds of laughter. When you say the word, 'laughter' or 'humour' it's like saying the word 'music' – there're all different branches. And right at the very bottom, of course, you get things like irony, sarcasm, satire and I think, the bitter laughter of defeat, hopelessness. But somewhere in between there's the most wonderful sound in the world. An audience laughing its head off. Humour can be very compassionate – you laugh sometimes because it just saves you from crying. Humour can be very compassionate.

Someone who took me completely by surprise was Dame Kiri Te Kanawa. Although not an opera lover myself I so much enjoyed her singing at the wedding of the Prince and Princess of Wales, and together with her recording of 'Blue Skies' with Nelson Riddle, I knew she was my kind of girl. Her British home is tucked away near a golf course in Surrey, well away from her nearest neighbour – although I am sure she is one person whose scales could only bring delight to the neighbours. Although I knew that she was part Maori it was only when I read the notes and the press cuttings that I realised she had been adopted. I also learned that she and her husband had adopted their two children. She spoke about this:

RR     Your two children are adopted. Do you think there are any special privileges and joys of having adopted children, rather than having natural ones?

KTK    I think that one should be very grateful that you are given two healthy, wonderful children in the first place, whether they be your own or adopted. I was adopted myself, so I – I really can't see any difference in life. I looked at my mother and that was my mother and I never, ever had the interest or the – I don't know, I was never a very inquisitive sort of person. I accepted life for what it was. If it dealt you a blow and you could fix it and make it turn to your advantage, whether it be a good experience or a bad experience and say, 'Well I won't try that again', so that's to your advantage. But I was given such a glorious life and I certainly wouldn't be sitting here talking to you if I hadn't been adopted.

The biggest surprise in the interview came when she talked about an outing she had with her daughter which somehow didn't quite fit the picture of one of the world's leading opera singers:

**RR**    Something that obviously delights you is your family, although I was terrified to read in one press cutting that your daughter, Antonia, took you roller-skating once. The thought of Dame Kiri Te Kanawa roller-skating frightens me.

**KTK**    In the unbelievable boom – you know the noise you hear, if there's a car next door and it's going 'schuum-oom-aar-oom-aar-oom' and you think, 'What is happening to that person's ears?' Well, it was one of those places.

**RR**    Was it?

**KTK**    Air-conditioned, this unbelievable music, and us roller-skating. It was the funniest thing I've ever done.

**RR**    Were you on your bottom any of the time . . .

**KTK**    I did have a small slip in the dark at one point, and came home with a nice bruise somewhere.

Listeners to Radio 4 are, of course, very familiar with the wit and wisdom of Rabbi Lionel Blue and readers of the Roman Catholic paper, *The Universe*, know him as a cook. On *Good Morning Sunday* we were able to combine both talents. When the *Good Morning Sunday* cookery book was published we used him as our expert on Jewish food, but long before that I had sampled his cooking in the home of cookery writer Evelyn Rose. This had been a fairly easy home to get into as Evelyn's daughter, Judi, was at the time a researcher on the programme. Lionel kept us very much amused, as along with Evelyn he prepared breakfast:

**RR**    Lionel, are you a natural cook or do you do it all from recipes?

**LB**    No, no, no, I'm a natural cook. I will never forget the time I tried to make some pastry and I followed the recipe absolutely exactly, but it kept on coming apart and looking like lace. Finally I said 'To Hell with it' and I just threw the whole dough, which was getting greyer and greyer, through the window and hit the dog which howled. But they never told me that you had to flour a rolling pin or the board, typically. And they often leave out, you know, the most basic things.

**RR**    Are you like Evelyn in your recipes, and make it absolutely plain what everyone's got to do?

**LB**    No, I – well, yes I do, but – the only thing is I'm much more of an improviser because I've had to be, because I've learnt a lot of cooking on a boat, you see. I used to go sailing a great deal, and I've never really – because I had a very moving sort of life – I've never really had the advantage, you know, of a lovely kitchen like Evelyn's, with all these gadgets and everything. I've always had to make do and mend, you know, on camping sites and goodness knows where else.

After the programme was over Lionel and I travelled back to London together. I was extremely glad of his company because on Sunday mornings the trains from Manchester to London always took the scenic route. On this occasion it seemed to be more scenic than ever with the journey taking nearly five and a half hours.

Most sports people were interviewed when I was away from the programme and it was being cared for by a guest presenter, especially if the presenter happened to be Chris Stuart. At a very early stage the producers realised that my knowledge of sport was somewhat limited (I try to be honest). I have never really been gripped by snooker, darts, golf or any physically active sports, and so as not to embarrass either myself or the interviewee, it became general policy to keep sports persons and me apart. There was, however, one tennis commentator I was able to talk to and this was because we had something other than tennis to talk about. Gerald Williams is a very committed Christian:

**RR** There is something that I know is incredibly important to you and that's your Christian faith.

**GW** Hmm-hmm.

**RR** Now has that always been part of your life?

**GW** No, no. I was brought up – we were three brothers – we were brought up to go to Church. Both my parents were very involved in our local Church and I sang in the choir and I was an altar-server – I was a boat boy.

**RR** This was very high Church.

**GW** Yes.

**RR** Smells and bells.

**GW** Yes – very high indeed. In a book I wrote I was a little ungenerous about the effect that had on my life, because I think in fact it must have had some effect. Although in the short term I think, the effect wasn't very positive. And so as I moved on in my career, heading irresistibly as I felt towards Fleet Street, going to Church became a spasmodic thing . . .

**RR** With no commitment attached to it at all?

**GW** Not really, no, not that I understood. I liked going to Church, but – but, no it didn't make a lot of difference to the lifestyle I led.

**RR** So what triggered the change?

**GW** I would say two things, although that's too simple, but we haven't got time to go into it more deeply. The outstanding thing was that my marriage broke up after eight years, and that was absolutely catastrophic. It was unthinkable, and it sort of left me with nothing. And a little before that, about five years before, I think, the other great influence was that at covering a tennis tournament for the *Daily Mail* in Manchester I had met a bloke who looked like a pub bouncer . . . and actually behaves rather like one to this day. He's a former Cambridge rugger player and his name is Alan Godson and he was a vicar of St Mary's Church in Toxteth – just outside Toxteth, in Liverpool. I had never met a Christian who was so physical and upfront and, un-churchey, and although a lot about what Alan said and did, like endlessly sending me paperbacks through the post, none of which I read at the time, a lot of Alan Godson was so provocative to me that I almost couldn't take him. Yet there was something about the man that I was fascinated by – his total commitment.

RR    Do you think he was challenging you, in any way?

GW    Oh, yes, not half – he challenges everybody. He led one of the church wardens of his Church to Christ up the ladder when the poor fellow came there to clean the windows at the vicarage. I mean, he's that kind of evangelist. But, you know, I always think people like that are a bit like a stick of rock. If you break a stick of rock you bought on the shorefront at Brighton, all the way through it'll say 'Brighton' . . .

RR    Yes.

GW    . . . and if you break people like Alan Godson all the way through it'll say 'Jesus Christ'; and in my hurt all those years ago he was the one telephone number I would ring.

Someone whom I'd always respected and long wanted to meet was the Cardinal Archbishop of Westminster, Cardinal Basil Hume. He first granted me an interview for the start of 1989. We had adopted a policy of trying to have a religious leader with whom to start the year. Having interviewed the Archbishop of Canterbury the previous year it was now the turn of the head of the Roman Catholics in this country to have his say. He is a man of great faith and dignity who very sensibly, like the Archbishop of Canterbury, makes sure that he has someone with him as a sounding board when he is doing an interview:

**RR**  It was quite an eventful 1988 for you, because I saw somewhere that your marriage was announced in '88. What happened there?

**CH**  I received a copy of Debrett's one morning and was quite astonished, because it's a very expensive book and I hadn't ordered it. I laid it aside and then later in the day, I found a letter next to it and it was deeply apologetic because they had married me off. I think somebody on the staff there had mistaken the fact that the Bishop of Guildford had got re-married, as a widower, in Westminster, and so got confused with Bishop and Westminster. I have had a fair amount of leg-pulling, as you can imagine.

**RR**  It sounds as though you dealt with it very sensibly though.

**CH**  Well, there was a side of me that rather enjoyed it!

He then went on to tell me about a very special, and in some ways very private, occasion that had happened at Westminster:

**RR**  When we were chatting before, you mentioned a very special day you shared in.

**CH**  Oh yes, it was an extraordinary event. Somebody – I can't remember quite who – had the idea of my preaching on a quiet day to men and women who have no home and spend the night living rough out of doors. They all came here and I preached a little sermon and then we went on pilgrimage into the Cathedral. We went to Our Lady's Altar and we prayed together. Then we went round the Stations of the Cross, the Stations which are showing the different events as Our Lord went up to Calvary for his death, and I just explained what each station is meant to be. And they were absolutely lovely – you really felt that they were people who by and large life has treated very hard, and they haven't had it easy. And, to be able to speak to them on how the Lord has tremendous compassion and love for them, it's – well, that's a priest's job – to tell people that.

The notes and the press cuttings that the researchers provided for me always made interesting reading. However, my greatest delight was when, during the interview, the interviewee was willing to share that little bit extra.

However, there were times when I felt that I had got nowhere. An interview that stayed at such a superficial level that by the end of the programme we knew little more than when we started was rare. Fortunately, because the interviews were never confrontational, most guests were prepared to reveal, if not all, at least a very generous amount of their feelings, their faith and their life in order to lighten the lives of those who heard them.

# PLACES OF PILGRIMAGE

Although some people don't approve of shrines or see any need for outward and visible signs to remind them of a transcendent God, a great number of people obviously do. Their faith is helped if they are able to concentrate their minds on something physical. To be able to look at a cross or a picture, to be able to light a candle or feel rosary beads, to be able to stand at the actual spot where it is thought something happened, is something which strengthens their faith, but is in no way a substitute for faith itself. With our visits to the Holy Land it was obvious that we were going to visit many places of pilgrimage. On my first visit there with the travellers on the cruise ship *Orpheus* it was wonderful to share, in person with some listeners, the reading of the Beatitudes from the Sermon on the Mount as we passed that Mount, crossing the Sea of Galilee on our way to Capernaum. In the Galilee area it was very easy to imagine Jesus attracting the crowd who came to listen to Him. From Bishop Jim Thompson I got his reaction.

**RR**   Jim, this is your first time into Galilee, isn't it?
**JT**   Yes, it's absolutely wonderful. We came across the sea this morning, we stopped in the middle and read the Sermon on the Mount as we could see the hill where the Sermon was meant to have been preached. Now we've come here to Capernaum where Peter and Andrew almost certainly lived, and there are fishing boats drawn up on the shore.

RR   And what are your feelings about this part of Israel?

JT   Well, I feel enormously closer to Jesus' life than perhaps in, say, Jerusalem where so much has changed. Here there's all the plant life, all the beauty around us that was here in Jesus' day.

RR   This was a very important place for Jesus, wasn't it?

JT   Indeed, it was a sort of headquarters of his ministry, and it's interesting that here in this lovely place you can see over there between the hills the route that Jesus would have come from Nazareth. So this was his – the place that he knew most. But even in this beautiful place, he experienced first of all the tremendous conflicts that were to come, because we're just near the fourth-century synagogue which perhaps was built on the site of an old synagogue which would have been the one in which Jesus taught. There he was thrown out of the synagogue because of the authority he claimed when he cast out the evil spirits. So even here, surrounded by this wonderful scene, he must have already known he was going to have a terrible time ahead of him.

RR   How important was the synagogue to Jesus?

JT   Our Jewish guide keeps on saying he was born as a Jew, brought up as a Jew, lived as a Jew, died as a Jew, so the synagogue was tremendously important. This was in a way a forerunner of what happened to the Church – they got into tremendous conflict, but Jesus called us to love and worship his Father, who was of course the God of the Jews. So I always hope and pray that the time will come that Jews and Christians will be able in some way to come together again.

Not all places of pilgrimage were quite as public. As we left Capernaum we travelled to Nazareth. Nazareth was somewhere that we had not featured on *Good Morning Sunday* before and yet, of course, it played an important part in Jesus' childhood. Tucked away in the back streets of this busy town is a community of nuns whose main work is to care for children with disabilities. But during the renovation of their house they discovered what they thought was the remains of a first-century house, the sort of house in which Mary, Joseph and the child Jesus would have lived. Sister Veronica Carthy told me about it:

RR    Now I hear through some marvellous cleaning you suddenly found that you were sitting on a treasure in a way, of a first-century house. Now, what sort of house is this? What's it like?

SV    Well, it's what remains of a very primitive house. The houses at that time were in fact grottos, they were dug into the rock itself and the people used the rock of the mountain and adapted them, made walls and made an entrance – a door. You have it here where you have a vertical hinge dug into the rock itself and in the wall you have a place where they must have put a bar or something to close that door.

RR    Now could this have been the sort of house that the Holy Family lived in?

SV    It could have been, yes, because it is from that time and we know that they did live in grottos in fact, and used one very big room – it used to be very dark, I believe, and they used to keep their oil lamps burning all day.

RR    Just one thing before I leave you – I believe there has been a fascinating tomb found nearby. When does that date from?

SV    It dates from the time, in fact, of the discovery of the house. The house and the tomb were discovered practically at the same time, we were building our church, we found two big lumps of stone covering a hole and when these stones were taken off, there was a very strong smell of incense, they say. They continued the excavations and found a very interesting tomb, because it is a Herodian tomb. That is you can place it fifty years before Christ, and fifty years afterwards.

**RR**    And who might be buried there?

**SV**    Well, that we don't know, because all we have is an aural tradition from the veneration of the tomb of the Just. Now we know that Joseph is called Just in the Bible, but he's not the only one so we have to be very prudent. But it could be his tomb, because there are apocryphal texts that say that Joseph died in Nazareth and was buried and describe his funeral. It's just a possibility that we have his tomb.

When travelling in the Middle East, especially with the two Swan Hellenic cruises, it was not only places connected with Jesus that we visited, we also visited many places which Paul had visited on his missionary journeys and on his final journey to Rome. But I think for me the most interesting place we visited was Patmos. This tiny Greek island is of course connected with the St John who wrote the Book of Revelation. It was a place that Mary O'Hara, the singer and harpist, had always wanted to visit having been told that from it she would derive great spiritual strength. On the isle of Patmos I asked Mary for her impressions of whether the visit had come up to expectation:

**MO'H**    I've been wanting to come to Patmos since 1974, my first visit to Greece – and now it's finally been realised. Why – because it's where the most, I think the most dynamic book in the Scripture comes from, and it's a sort of culmination of the whole message. And although it's a book of horrors – it's also a book of great beauty. And it has this ending which to me gives total meaning to life, which is longing for the Perusia – it ends with the cry *'Maranatha.* Come, Lord Jesus!' This is why I wanted to come to Patmos because this is what makes sense of everything in one's life. To be where actually the Revelation was made, is something quite exceptional.

**RR**   It's a great challenging book as well, though, isn't it?

**MO'H**   It is, yes, it is. It's also a very encouraging book, it tells them they've been very badly behaved *but*; and of course the paramount message is perseverance.

**RR**   Of course, St John was originally here because he was a prisoner, wasn't he, on a prison island.

**MO'H**   That's right, yes.

**RR**   Do you feel that at all as you've walked round?

**MO'H**   Well, I certainly find you look at it, and it is very hilly. And when you mount to what is probably the topmost area of the island and you look down and see this grim coastline, it's an apt enough place for a penal settlement. That's what it was all about, wasn't it – his banishment to this place of probably hard labour and certainly of isolation. I remember thinking when we were mounting some of these very steep steps and hills, who knows, he may have been one of the many prisoners who laid the original paths of what we are now walking on.

One Easter we travelled to County Wicklow in Ireland to visit the Glen Cree reconciliation centre. This place has become a place of pilgrimage for all those who want to see Christians living together in peace and harmony. We did the actual broadcast from one of those beautifully decorated horse-drawn caravans in which many people spend their holidays in Ireland. We were fortunate to have with us the caravan owner's son, Cillian, otherwise we would never have been able to get the horse in the shafts, let alone encouraged it to the place outside the centre from which we hoped to do the broadcast.

This broadcast had about it all the warmth and friendliness that you associate with the Emerald Isle. It also had an element of confusion. The hotel in which we stayed was more used to the casual visitor, rather than the working broadcaster, so little essentials like telephones in the bedrooms didn't exist. An element of tension had even broken out between one of the producers and the landlady. It seems as though she was unable to understand what was really required when he asked for his eggs to be hard boiled.

With doing the programme on Easter Day it was essential that we were over there for Good Friday as well. Officially the hotel was shut on that day, and although we had informed the landlady that we were going out and our expected time of return, we found ourselves locked out. Fortunately, by exploring one of the fire escapes we found a window that was open and so made our entrance that way. It may well be, of course, that the landlady was not that keen on our returning because when, on Holy Saturday, I told her that one of the team was leaving to return to London she threw up her hands in sheer delight and said 'Oh, Holy Mary, one of them's going, how marvellous, how marvellous.' It really did sound as though one of her prayers had been answered.

Later that Easter Eve we faced a problem which could have been extremely serious. We all went to bed happy in the knowledge that all the preparation that could be done had been done. At 2 a.m. the landlady woke us up. One of our cars had been stolen. It was the one which contained much equipment that we would need later that morning. The police were called and fortunately, through natural intelligence, they said that they had a very good idea where the car would be. They drove us to a wood where we were just in time to see the equipment being off-loaded into a getaway car. The mounties may always be known for getting their man but it is obvious that this gift is also possessed by the Garda.

Remembrance Sunday was a most important day for the listeners to *Good Morning Sunday* as well as the viewers of *Songs of Praise*. One particularly moving *Songs of Praise* that I was associated with was the one which linked the ruins of Coventry Cathedral with the rebuilt Cathedral in Dresden. Both cities had suffered greatly in the bombing and both cities have become places of pilgrimage for those who felt that we needed to be reminded of the horrors of war and its futility. Cliff Michelmore was in the cathedral in Dresden, while I got soaked in the pouring rain with a large crowd of people in the ruins of Coventry.

The German and British people sang together, sometimes in one another's language, showing that reconciliation had taken place and prayed the prayer of Coventry 'Father Forgive'. On both sides we heard of people's experiences and I particularly remember some of the things I was told, especially by Ken Turner:

**RR**    Ken Turner was the Town Clerk of Coventry's right hand man in 1940.

**KT**    It took me an hour and a half to get to work instead of twenty minutes because of being diverted all over the place. So, when I got to the centre of the city, it was obvious the damage, although there had been considerable high explosive damage, was mostly due to fire. A lot of the buildings were on fire, and the Fire Brigade was standing there with their hoses flat, unable to do anything about it, because all the water supplies had been interrupted with bombs.

**RR**    Ken, you've lived in Coventry all your life. What were your feelings to see your city in ruins?

**KT**    I really was devastated. Probably what would illustrate it as much as anything – I walked past the church that I had attended ever since I was a child, to go to work and that church no longer existed. And this was a blow, a complete shattering blow to me. I wouldn't have believed it could have affected me in that way, but it did.

**RR**    Do you think you could ever forgive the Nazis the suffering they rained on Coventry?

**KT**    Oh yes, I think so. I'm very reminded of the then Provost, Provost Howard, who on Christmas Day 1940, which was only about four or five weeks after the raid, standing in the ruins of his Cathedral and broadcasting to the Empire as it was – 'We are trying, hard as it may be, to banish all thoughts of revenge. We are bracing ourselves to finish this tremendous job of saving the world from tyranny and cruelty. We are going to try to make a kinder, simpler, a more Christ-Child like sort of world in the days beyond this strife.' And in the months that followed, he made it clear that what he was really saying was, 'Father, forgive us all, not just the Germans.' 'Father, forgive us all' in terms of man's inhumanity to man.

On *Good Morning Sunday* we made a great effort to respect people's feelings on Remembrance Sunday as well as, hopefully, stressing the need for peace and the wastefulness of war. On one occasion I travelled with General Sir John Hackett to re-live his memories of Arnhem. He had been with the paratroopers there. The fighting had been fierce and many of the forces had paid a sacrificial price for being there. One of the most memorable moments of that programme was when we reunited Sir John with the Dutch family who had sheltered him:

**RR**     After his life had been saved by skilful surgery at St Elizabeth's Hospital, Sir John was ready to escape back to the country. However, his physical condition was in no way fit enough to allow him to try, so he was hidden and nursed by a Dutch Christian family in the little town of Ede. By chance, their house was next door to where the German military police were billeted, so at very great personal risk the family not only hid him from the occupying German forces but they treated him as one of the family. So it was obviously with enormous pleasure that Sir John came with us again to Ede to meet two members of that family, Dr John Snoek and his sister, Mary. They had played a major part in nursing him back to health and in his subsequent escape. But hadn't they been afraid of the consequences of being found with an Allied soldier in their home?

**JS**     I remember that at certain moments when it was

not justified to be afraid I was shivering all over, and at other moments when we should have been terribly afraid we just felt relaxed. Perhaps that saved us in many respects because somehow you communicate to others your fear, and we were walking in the streets and were not afraid.

MS Can I add something? I think one of the primary feelings then was not to be afraid, but to be very proud and say, one of the liberators is in our house and the Germans don't know it. So before when I saw a German, I was very angry, but then when I saw him I smiled to him, thinking, 'Ha, ha, I know something you don't know!'

RR But you were at risk.

JS Sometimes we were terribly afraid, yes.

RR Do you think it was helped by the fact that your home was very much a Christian home?

JS Yes and no. In those days I was over-critical of the Christian set-up and I still am – still very critical.

RR And you're now a minister?

JS Yes. But in those days I had trouble fighting my way into the community, because I often felt that we did not live up to the challenge of the Christian faith. But I think we realised that we were in God's hands, though we also realised that sometimes people believing and trusting in God have to suffer and be murdered. Even so, we would have trusted that we just had to do what we had to do according to our conscience.

MS If you stop and think about all these things which can happen you dare to do nothing. You are too afraid. And so it is much better not to think too much.

RR John, I believe there used to be a bit of hymn singing in this home. How did that go?

JS Well, in those days we used as families to sing around a harmonium. Nowadays there are many that laugh at that, and I must confess that in our home it is not as central as it was. But we discovered that the hymn 'Abide With Me' had a great meaning to Sir John and his regiment, because in the eighteenth century his regiment in Spain misbehaved and since then they have always had to sing 'Abide With Me' after the national anthem. He told us and so we used the hymn on his birthday.

RR    Sir John, is this true about your regiment?

SJ    Yes it is. The playing of 'Abide With Me' after the regimental march was enjoined upon my regiment as a punishment for some, may I say, indifferent behaviour, I believe in a convent somewhere abroad. And we do it to this day. We always follow it with a rousing little tune about being a galloping Irish Hussar but we sing 'Abide With Me' every time the national anthem is played.

In 1988 I went to Belgium for the seventieth anniversary of the end of the First World War. It was most moving to stand by the Menin Gate in Ypres at the eleventh hour on the eleventh day of the eleventh month, remembering in silence those who had died and those who had suffered. For that Remembrance Sunday we based ourselves in Poperinge at the house the Reverend Tubby Clayton used as his headquarters for TocH. It still welcomes many visitors whose links with TocH go back to the war years and who still make regular pilgrimages to the war graves.

In the attic of the house, which was the chapel, I talked with Colin Rudd about the work of TocH:

RR    The Reverend Colin Rudd and I have come right to the top of Talbot House, here in Poperinge to what in fact, Colin, is a very special room.

CR    Yes it is. This is the loft and in this beautiful old house the loft used to be the place where hops were hung to dry before they were used to make the local beer. When the house became a rest centre for Allied troops coming back from the front line in the Ypres Salient in 1915, young men from the

Westminster Rifle Brigade turned the loft into a chapel, this upper room, which became the heart of the house. To this upper room came young men of all ranks and of none, to find a quiet place where they could think and pray. Here was a place where some of them, at least, would return, many seeking comfort in sorrow at the death or maiming of friends, and to give thanks for their own safety.

But Talbot House wasn't simply a place of comfort – there was challenge here, too. The Reverend Philip Clayton, or 'Tubby' as he was known to his countless friends, an army chaplain who opened and ran the centre, was deeply convinced of the unique value of each human person. This was a house where *all* were welcomed – it was Everyman's Club – and that not out of any vague sense of general goodwill to all, but out of a firm Christian belief that we are all created in the image of God, and that there's nothing about us that's more important than that. The challenge that was here was to dare to meet others at a level which went beyond the merely superficial, breaking down barriers of rank and background. Those who met that challenge found a depth of fellowship which, for many, was even deeper than that which they found in the trenches.

The house stands today not simply as a memorial to those who came here during those terrible years, nor is it just another First World War museum. Although both of those things are part of its life, its main role now is to be a centre for reconciliation and peace, and to bear witness to the need for both in modern society.

No visit to this part of Europe would have been complete without paying my respects to those who had died serving this country, fighting for our freedom. The war graves are kept beautifully but as you wander amongst the headstones you realise what a costly thing war is. Row upon row of graves of mainly young men stood as witnesses to war's destructive power. As I visited the cemetery at Tyne Cot I had this to say:

**RR**     We have been to the sites of fighting, to Talbot House and now we've come to one of the largest cemeteries here on the Western Front, where in fact eleven thousand, nine hundred people are buried. It's Tyne Cot, the scene of the Battle of Passchendaele, and it's amazing as I look out over the cemetery, you see row upon row upon row of graves, with the flowers and the plants in between, easing the solemnness of all those white stones. And it's quite amazing because although there are crowds of people here as you doubtless can hear yourselves, and farm machinery in the background, there's a peace, there's a tranquillity, there's a tremendous dignity, there's a silence that broods over this place through the mist, and points to us the fact that so many people gave their lives so that we could live in freedom.

And it's interesting – I managed to take a look at the Visitors' Book as I came in through the gate, and there's Ian Buchanan from London, and one from Redhill in Surrey, saying 'We must never forget' and how absolutely true that is. A youngster here, Mark Budd, it looks like, from Rainham in Kent, who says: 'Always remembered' – very touching. It's very good when a youngster is saying that. Another youngster writing here, Greg Smith, also from Rainham, says: 'War is unnecessary'.

We also visited some of the scenes of battle themselves and I saw the conditions under which men had to fight. Trenches dug out of the ground gave very little cover against bullets and shells which were exploding all around them. At Hill 62 I saw the very close quarters at which the men were forced to fight:

**RR**     I have come to Hill 62, which was regarded as the Clapham Junction of this part of the Western Front

*91*

and with me is Mervyn Smith from Galloway Travel who has brought a crowd of kids here this morning. Mervyn, good morning to you.

MS     Good morning.

RR     Now where would the Germans actually have been here?

MS     At the moment we're nearly on the tip of the Salient, so the Germans would have actually been on three sides of us, coming from just the east side of Passchendaele, which would have been over in that direction, and then coming from, totally from the east, from Menin, and also from the southern part, coming from Mesen.

RR     Now are these genuine trenches, or have they been dug out as a memorial?

MS     No these trenches are all genuine and totally untouched. As you can see over there, there are still bullet holes in the sides of the trenches that happened throughout the war.

RR     They must have been appalling conditions, I mean, look at the mud.

MS     That's right. Sometimes we have the children come back to the coach literally waist high in mud.

RR     And what about down to my left – there's this tunnel here which seems to be full of water.

MS     This tunnel would actually have been used to give you a connection from one trenchline to another trenchline which was way over to our left.

RR     What about that colossal shell we spotted just over there?

MS     That's right. I mean, all around this area all the time you see farmers pulling out shells even now, to this day, and a lot of it is just left there for people to see the remains from the war.

RR     Now these trees, would they have offered protection to the soldiers who were here?

MS     Well, they would have done at the beginning probably. But as you can see, there's just lots of stubs left. They are riddled with bullet holes and

92

lumps of them have been chopped away by the shells. So they wouldn't obviously, after a while, have made any cover at all.

Many people may think that the Cabinet War Room is an odd place to consider as a place of pilgrimage but for some people it definitely is. Dug deep under the buildings of Whitehall is the place where decisions were made in secrecy and in relative security. The custodians of the War Rooms, which are fascinating to visit, allowed me to do my broadcast actually sitting at Churchill's desk.

If the War Rooms were considered a strange place of pilgrimage to some, a visit to Lourdes would be considered by many a natural place for pilgrimage. Lourdes in southern France is where Bernadette had her frequent visions of the Virgin Mary and it is at the spring and the shrine that it is claimed miraculous healings have taken place.

The *Good Morning Sunday* team joined the pilgrimage that was being led by Cardinal Basil Hume. It was quite a long journey by air and road but on the coach journey I talked to two ladies and a priest. One of the ladies visited Lourdes on several occasions, for the other this was her first visit:

**RR**    Connie, this isn't your first visit to Lourdes, is it?

**C**    No, it's about my twentieth.

**RR**    Why is Lourdes so special for you?

**C**    There's an atmosphere here that you never find anywhere else, an atmosphere of prayer and devotion, and it's most outstanding amongst the sick – they're so patient and so full of gratitude for everything that is done for them.

**RR**    Well, I'm looking forward to that and someone else who'll be looking forward to it is Josephine, because Josephine, this *is* your first visit, isn't it?

**J**    Yes, it is. I've never been before.

**RR**    Now why have you come on this trip?

**J**    Well, firstly I came to accompany Connie because we both go to the same Church.

**RR**    Which is?

J St Edmund Campion in Maidenhead. And I thought it would be a marvellous opportunity to come to Lourdes.

RR Are you a sick person?

J No I'm not, but I have a grandson who's got cystic fibrosis, so I thought I would come for his sake.

RR And you'll be upholding him in your prayers?

J Oh yes, yes.

RR Marvellous. And Father, over here, obviously it's not the first time for you, is it?

F No, I come almost every year with the Diocese of Brentwood on pilgrimage. I think that the main thing that I enjoy about it is that all the emphasis is naturally given to sick people, but this enables each of us to realise that we are all in need of healing – not just those whom we are taking in stretchers to the grotto but every pilgrim can receive a great sense, I think, of strengthening and encouragement.

When we arrived in the town of Lourdes itself I had grave doubts about the whole exercise. I realised that there was bound to be a commercial side to such a place but I don't think I had reckoned on it being quite so big. Shop after shop sold religious souvenirs, some tasteful, some to my way of thinking lacked any taste whatsoever. I have never seen such hideous statues of the Virgin Mary and I am not sure that she would like to be used as a water bottle.

The scene changes, however, when you move away from the town and arrive at the area which is called the Domain. In this area no commercial enterprise is allowed whatsoever and you do feel that the people are there for one purpose only, and that is to pray. At the site of the grotto, where Bernadette had her visions, an altar has been set up and on this occasion the celebrant and preacher was Cardinal Basil Hume. The engineer who came with us had brought enough equipment to wire the whole area for sound. I think he thought he was going to record the service à la Radio 3's

*Choral Evensong.* All we needed, in fact, was a snippet of the service so as to capture the atmosphere.

In Lourdes you are surrounded by the sick and it concerned me that people may have been given false hopes about their visit. So I spoke to someone about the verification of miracles that it was claimed had taken place there:

RR     Since people have been coming here about five thousand pilgrims have claimed to be cured, and each one has had to pass stringent medical scrutiny at the Medical Bureau. That's where I am now, and with me is Doctor Jack Douglas who is the retired Chief Medical Officer of the Society of Our Lady of Lourdes. Doctor Jack, very nice to meet you. And I hear you're not feeling too well, so this is kind of you.

JD     Thank you very much.

RR     Of these five thousand cures, how many have been officially classed as miracles?

JD     Only sixty-four.

RR     Why is it so few?

JD     Because at the beginning of the miraculous events happening in Lourdes, since 1858, there was no documentation. People came along with various diseases, obviously infections, particularly things like tuberculosis which was a common condition then. And these people got up and left their crutches behind and proclaimed they were cured. Well, they may have been serious diseases, they may not. But the point is that there was no documentary evidence of this happening – of there being a true cure, which scientific principles, knowledge of doctors could explain.

RR     So what demands do you make on a person to make sure it is a miraculous cure?

JD     If a person thinks that they can walk, say, whereas previously they were in a chair, they declare themselves to the Medical Bureau in Lourdes which is run by Doctor Mangiapan, and he will ask all the doctors who happen to be in the area on pilgrimages to attend. He has a conference set up that day, within an hour or two and the patient is examined. Notes are made as to what the patient was like before and what the patient is like now after the claim has been made of their cure.

RR    So it is very thorough indeed.

JD    Very thorough.

RR    When does the Church become involved in this?

JD    The Church becomes involved when – if – all the doctors come to the conclusion that this cannot be explained medically.

RR    Now to have a cure, does it mean that someone has actually been dipped in the waters by the grotto?

JD    Not necessarily. But one of the conditions is that it must be an immediate cure. In other words, the thing must happen at the time that they are in Lourdes, within a few minutes or an hour or two, or a day or so. And it must be permanent.

RR    Doctor, I believe you have got a specific example about someone from Liverpool that you have been particularly interested in. Who is that?

JD    A man called John Traynor who was a soldier in the First World War. In 1914 he had a shrapnel injury to his head and a year later, 1915, in Gallipoli he received very severe gunshot wounds. Following that he became completely paralysed with one arm, he also had trouble with his head, he had fits, he couldn't walk, and he became a hundred per cent incapacitated. He was granted a hundred per cent pension. He came to Lourdes and – I'm not sure if it was the first time or the second time – he got up from the chair and said 'I can walk' and he walked back from the station in Lime Street in Liverpool and that evidence was given me by a patient of mine, who was a non-Catholic, and said 'I remember that fellow. I saw him being carried out on a stretcher and I saw him walk back from the train.' The interesting thing was that he applied to have his pension taken away from him and the Department of Health and Social Security could not do it because there was no machinery available for taking back a hundred per cent disability pension!

One visit I made was to the hospital in the Domain. Here I met some remarkable people. One lady I talked to, Margaret Smith-Galer, was only too pleased to be able to tell me what Lourdes meant to her:

**RR**    Margaret, nice to meet you.

**MS-G**  Nice to meet you, Roger.

**RR**    Where exactly do you come from?

**MS-G**  I come from Epping in Essex.

**RR**    Now you had a brain haemorrhage eight years ago?

**MS-G**  Yes.

**RR**    You've come through that?

**MS-G**  Yes.

**RR**    But you've got multiple sclerosis, now.

**MS-G**  Yes.

**RR**    So what in fact does Lourdes mean to you?

**MS-G**  What it means to me – I come to renew my faith because when a person is sick, they are inclined at times to indulge in self-pity – why should it be us, you know? And, when you come to Lourdes, for one week you are with a family, it's one big family, you see people who have come here, unpaid, who are more devoted than you'll ever find in the world, and they treat us as though – well, we're their children, really.

**RR**    Now one of the things I've noticed is there is nothing depressing about this ward.

**MS-G**  Nobody is depressed in Lourdes. You won't see anybody – you won't see a dying patient depressed, in Lourdes.

**RR**    You're a right lot of gigglers in a way, aren't you?

**MS-G**  That's right. We love Lourdes.

**RR**    Now why do you think there is this atmosphere?

MS-G   Because Our Lady has brought us here to be happy
       and to rejoice with her. We are rejoicing with her
       while we're here.
RR     But doesn't it worry you, Margaret, the thought
       that you might go home to Epping, here from
       Lourdes, without your MS cured?
MS-G   No, certainly not. I go home a much nicer person
       from Lourdes.

This wasn't the first time I'd heard about someone being
helped and strengthened by a visit to Lourdes. When I did a
*Songs of Praise* from St Chad's Roman Catholic Cathedral in
Birmingham, Bridget Hogan had this to say to me:

Well I imagined a great big swimming pool – you know – they
say 'the baths'. It wasn't, it was a small cubicle and there were
these French ladies telling me to get undressed, you see. So I
started doing it myself but she was going 'Sit, sit', so I sat,
and she helped me get my clothes off and then they put a
blue cloak around me and we walked to a pair of blue
curtains, and I stayed there. And I could hear this woman
there going 'Oh Jesus, Oh Mary' and she was crying her
eyes out, and I thought 'My God, what are they doing
to her?' I was literally shivering, not with cold but with
fright; so they brought me in and there were steps going
down to a stone bath, and two ladies held my wrists on either
side, and she said 'Remember your Baptism, and remember
what you wanted to ask Our Lady, and then make a good
sign of the Cross, and descend into the bath.' And when I
got actually into the bath, the water was up to my knees and
it was so cold, it was burning. By the time I had walked to
the end of the bath and kissed Our Lady's statue, my feet
and legs were burning, so they asked me could I sit, and I
said 'No, I'm sorry'. Can you kneel? I said no, so they
stooped me into the water and they poured water over me,
and I walked out. And I thought – I don't believe this – not
shuffling, I was walking, not very well, but I walked out.
The Sister saw me and she said 'I thought you had been
cured' and I said 'Well I don't know, Martha – my legs are

on fire, they're burning.' It wasn't till I came home again that I realised that that was a bit like being baptised again, you know, being born again actually, and I realised that God doesn't send things to you but in a way it opened my eyes to how I had sort of pushed him to one side because in the depths of my despair I was crying out, 'Take it away from me', I kept thinking, 'Take it away'. And I was lying in bed crying my eyes out with the pain, and yet in the back of my mind I kept thinking, Jesus said that in Gethsemane – 'but not my will but Yours' – so I used to stop and I would think: Well, yes, you know, I am united with Him in this suffering.

Many people are sceptical about such places. They feel that they encourage superstition. There may, of course, be an element of superstition in people's minds, but the vast majority of the people I met, talked to, and prayed with were people of great faith.

There is a shrine in Britain which is dedicated to Our Lady and is revered by Anglicans and Roman Catholics alike. It is at Walsingham in Norfolk. Daphne Tinsley told me something about the shrine and the pilgrims when I visited it for *Songs of Praise*:

**DT**    Some ask about the history of the shrine – how it was destroyed and how it was restored. Others ask how they can pay for a lamp to be lit for a relative who has died or somebody they love. Sometimes it is even more; you listen to people's problems and you show them where they can make intercessions – write their intercessions out. It is a place of prayer and a place of healing. It is a place steeped in history. From 1061, pilgrims have been coming here and there is a very special atmosphere. People, when they come in, remark about it. Only the other day, a young lady said 'Oh, the warmth in this place; there's something special here.'

**RR**    Now I saw a sign which said 'Sprinkling at 2.30'. What's involved in that?

**DT**    Well, at a sprinkling, the pilgrims go down the steps to the well and receive the water on their forehead, in their mouth, and in their hands, having first of all made an act of penitence. And then they go into the holy house for prayers, and then candles – we can light a candle as a special prayer – as a prayer for somebody who's in great pain, or for some great problem. So often we find that we cannot help people; there is nothing we can do for them, but we can light a candle and it symbolises our prayers to God.

The atmosphere at Walsingham was one of great joy and prayer. The sick had not gathered there in the same way as they had gathered at Lourdes and when I visited the Roman Catholic shrine the Archbishop of Liverpool, Derek Warlock, told me of a very special pilgrimage that had taken place soon after the last war:

**DW**    The people who decided to come on this pilgrimage were largely ex-servicemen whose mates had been killed, who were concerned about their families and they wanted a great kind of demonstration of faith for peace by penance and by prayer. And so from fourteen different parts of the country they started with fourteen crosses, weighing about 90 lbs apiece, and in groups of about twenty to thirty and from different starting places they converged on this little shrine of Our Lady of Walsingham.

    I was with Cardinal Griffin at the time as his chaplain, and as we approached Walsingham, we found to our surprise that all these little roads here were absolutely blocked with people and abandoned vehicles, and about a mile away we had to abandon the car ourselves and pick up the ecclesiastical impedimenta and make our way into the village. As we got to the Slipper Chapel, we found that far from being fully dressed, as were we, in all the archiepiscopal glory, the pilgrims with their heavy-weight crosses were in battle dress blouses. They were going to go bare foot down the holy mile, and I can remember that when eventually we came in procession into Walsingham itself, I was having to lean down over the Cardinal's long, flowing, scarlet silken train and remove from it bits of sticking plaster which had come off the blistered feet of the people who were walking in front of us. Yet it didn't seem strange because it was very much a time for penance.

**RR**  So how do you feel now, forty years on?

**DW**  In some ways, more than forty years older, but very conscious of the change – a change in society – and a change within the Church. People come to Walsingham not on a denominational basis – it isn't just ours, as it were. This has become increasingly a place where people can come to pray; people with faith and, in some cases, people who don't even know that they have faith. It's good that this ancient part of our heritage should be shared amongst all the people of this land.

In my early days of presenting *Good Morning Sunday* I was taken on a rather special pilgrimage. It was to the Derbyshire village of Tissington. Here each year at about Ascensiontide the villagers take the trouble to dress the wells with flowers. It is a custom which appears to be exclusive to Derbyshire.

The custom apparently, according to Roy Christian, originated in pagan sacrifices to water gods as a thanksgiving for past supplies and an inducement for further favours. The theory is that the Romans brought the custom to Derbyshire.

It was the religious significance of today's well dressing that interested us. The Early Church had been sensitive in the ways they handled pagan customs but in 960 there was a decree which expressly forbade the worship of fountains, although as late as 1102 St Anselm was still condemning this form of idolatry. Today the vast majority of the wells that are dressed are given a Christian theme. The Good Shepherd, the

Good Samaritan, and various hymns, such as 'Fight the Good Fight' and 'All Things Bright and Beautiful', make very popular themes that are represented.

When I arrived in the village I saw only the finished work and what works of art they all were. As I chatted to some of the people who had designed and built the displays I realised the tremendous amount of work that went into each one. Once the theme had been decided upon the construction of the display could begin. A frame had to be made which, after it had been soaked in the village pond, was covered with clay and had to be well puddled. The design was put on to this puddled clay and then the work began to cover it with greenery and flowers.

Roy Christian in his booklet, *Well Dressing in Derbyshire*, records that the dressers at Wirksworth Well in 1982 did a time and motion study to produce the following figures:

80 people worked 400 hours
Checking 3,000 nails on a frame
Puddling a quarter of a ton of clay
Using 10 cups of salt in the clay
They stuck on to the clay to make the pictures:
   3 buckets of parsley
   3 buckets of spurge
   7 jars of seeds
   10 yards of cones
   3,500 leaves
   3,800 bits of corn
   10,000 petals.

They had also drunk innumerable cups of coffee and raised two hundred pounds for charity.

At the time of the well dressing there is an ecumenical service held in the local church. At Tissington the church was packed and the service was relayed to those who were unable to get inside. By capturing the atmosphere of this event for *Good Morning Sunday* I hope we encouraged others to make the same pilgrimage as we made.

Pilgrimage is not, of course, restricted to visiting special places. In the New Testament it is made clear that any who wish to follow Jesus must make the whole of life a pilgrimage. But I think that you only realise the general when you stop and study the particular. All the pilgrimages that we made on *Good Morning Sunday* helped me and I hoped I helped the listeners to realise this.

# AWAYDAYS

As well as visiting those places which come readily to mind when thinking of doing religious broadcasts we also took ourselves off on more secular awaydays. During the summer we thought it would be good to visit some of Britain's holiday resorts and capture something of the atmosphere. After all, holidays started out as being Holy Days so we reasoned that a little trip to the seaside would do us all the world of good. These trips were particularly enjoyed by housebound listeners. Denied of a day out themselves they were able, metaphorically, to don their Kiss-Me-Quick hats, roll up their trouser legs, cover their heads with a knotted handkerchief and breathe in some of the bracing seaside air.

It wasn't just *Good Morning Sunday* that went out and about in the summer. *Songs of Praise* also packed its bags, left behind the cathedrals, chapels and churches, and headed for the great outdoors. The very first *Songs of Praise* that I did was in Eastbourne on the seafront. More often than not if the programme was at the coast, the lifeboat was near at hand. Not in its professional capacity, I hasten to add, but because people always liked a shot of a lifeboat and it was good public relations for the RNLI in their constant need to collect money.

Aberystwyth was another port of call for *Songs of Praise*. Here, because of time, I was helicoptered in. Helicopters and I don't really go together, I feel much safer in something a little larger with in-flight movies and waitress service; but at least I've learnt how to get out of a helicopter in the James Bond style – I have a photograph to prove it.

When you are recording in the open air there are so many extra hazards. Those responsible for recording the sound of the singing have a far harder job, even keeping everybody together isn't easy. At Aberystwyth we had the extra help of a researcher with severely impaired hearing Kerena Marchant's hearing dog, Skipper. Wherever Kerena goes so does Skipper, and naturally not only does he get to know the interviewees but more often than not they become his friends. So when we needed to gather all the interviewees together Skipper assumed the role of a sheepdog and rounded them all up.

Skipper made particular friends with one family:

**RR** Carol and Elved Evans run a lively pub in Aberystwyth. Their son, Sam, has suffered two major illnesses. The first brought about his deafness.

**CE** He had meningitis when he was nine months old, and it was as a result of that, that left him deaf.

**RR** And how did this affect him?

**CE** Well, it was a long time before we found out. It wasn't confirmed until he was two years and three months old.

**RR** Carol, what happened with the second illness?

**CE** He went in for a tonsil operation at the beginning of March, and about nine hours after the operation his heart virtually stopped, and he went into a coma and was unconscious. We didn't expect him to recover. They thought that the brain damage would be so severe that, even if he managed to pull through, there would be very little life for him.

**RR** Well, he is a very bright sparkling lad now, so how did he pull through?

**CE** We can only explain it by everybody's prayers, because there was no medical explanation at all. There was nothing they could do medically for him and we just had to hope and pray.

**RR** Was it just you as a family praying or was there other support?

CE    The whole town and beyond and from all over the world really. Our own vicar came up to the hospital every day. We had Communion at the hospital which helped us a great deal. The headmaster phoned round all the other schools in the area and all the schools were praying for him as well.

RR    Did the children do anything else to help?

CE    The children in his class sang all the songs that he knew. Mrs Griffiths read a story and we used to play that tape to him just afterwards. No reaction at all. The days went by. It was as though he could hear something. Perhaps a lot of people were praying for a full recovery but in some ways I couldn't hope for as much as that. It was so hopeless at one stage, and then he started to make improvements and it was as though he was determined that he was going to fight every inch of the way, so of course we just had to and we were praying then for every little bit of improvement and, well, he's just the same as he was before.

RR    How do you see the future for Sam?

CE    We are really getting back to starting him talking in phrases and sentences again now, and we had his school report yesterday which was a lovely report.

RR    It was good news, was it?

CE    'About the only word I can say to describe Sam is "remarkable" '. We thought that that was very very nice, and that they 'looked forward to every new step in his development' and that is how we feel now.

Not all the awaydays for *Songs of Praise* were at seaside resorts, although I do remember a visit to Brighton which ended with the most beautiful sunset just as we were singing 'The Day Thou Gavest Lord has Ended'.

Sometimes it was an open-air site which had historic significance. Ruins and I seem to go together and so I was not surprised to find myself doing a programme from the ruins of Ludlow Castle in Shropshire. The weather was terrible. It was so bad that we had to return a second day to complete the hymn singing but the people seemed to be able to keep smiles on their faces. This was thanks mainly to Roy Massey, the person responsible for music at Hereford Cathedral. He created and kept a wonderful atmosphere which helped people to enjoy themselves while he got the best out of them musically. He also disciplined us well. As soon as he gave the signal umbrellas had to be taken down and were not allowed up again until he gave the command.

Islington is certainly no holiday resort nor does its Green make claims to much that is historically significant. But it was on this Green that we did one of the open-air *Songs of Praise*. I had never realised what a cosmopolitan area it is. The programme started with a moving procession organised by the Italian Christians of the area. Kurdish refugees were being cared for in a United Reform Church and a black-led Church with many of its members having come originally from Nigeria, helping to make up a great tapestry of Christian believers.

The other thing that fascinated me about this programme was an interview I did with two men in one of the many antique shops of the area. Ashe Choudry and David Ludwick sold bubble wrap and this they used as a way of preaching the Gospel:

**RR**    Ashe Choudry and David Ludwick sell bubble wrap and other packaging items to the shopkeepers. I met them in the shop of one of their customers, Val Cooper, who has an antique business in the Angel Arcade. Are you selling anything as well as the bubble wrap?

**AC**    Well, not sort of selling but if an opportunity arises at Camden Passage to talk about the Lord Jesus, then we take it.

**RR**    Serving him by selling bubble wrap can seem a contradiction in terms.

**DL**    Well, God has got a wonderful sense of humour.

**AC**    St Paul, I think he was a tent maker.

**RR**    You could be making much more money if you were doing a regular job. Why do you do this one?

**DL**    Well, it's not all about money. Yes, we need money to live, obviously, and we have our expenses but it's the joy we get out of it and the results we see. One of the girls last week came up to us, just outside here actually, and said 'Oh David, you know I've been meaning to have a word with you,' and she just gave me a list of friends she wanted us to pray for. We get the odd occasion where you get the odd shout or this or that or 'Get out of it' but nothing like Christians get in other countries. I would also like to say it's good for us to be here because we have a right to be in the market because we give a service. We have our business to run and we have the other side, which is about the Lord Jesus and people ask us lots of questions – 'Where do you get your joy from?' – and that is a tremendous opportunity. Sometimes they say 'What have you been drinking or what sort of drugs have you been taking?' and we say 'Nothing, but you know, if you really want to know, you don't have to wait until you die to have the fun and the joy and the good time. You are sort of experiencing eternal life now.'

I also spent a very enjoyable day in another part of London. The programme was being recorded in Rathbone Market in the London Borough of Newham. This is real East End country so I was very glad to have with me the actress Anna Wing who at the time was playing Lou Beale in the television soap opera *EastEnders*. She is a great person who I'd met before on *Good Morning Sunday* and it was obvious that the crowd was pleased to see her. We actually sang one of the hymns to the *EastEnders* signature tune.

Amongst those who were interviewed was a Tamil family. The East End has always been home to people from all over the world and it was good to be able to find out how the latest arrivals were settling in. So as to try and make them feel at home we sang one of the hymns in Tamil. A little bit of instruction was needed but east enders are very adaptable. At the end of that hymn I joined two of the congregation, Benny and Alan. Benny admitted he didn't understand a word of it but he certainly enjoyed himself. Before we recorded the hymns I had met them and they gave me a fascinating interview:

AY One afternoon, me and me friend was finishing off a bottle of Johnnie Walker's and I popped out for a little while to the front door, and there was Nigel Copsie, a priest, walking along, and so I asked him if he wanted a drink, and he said 'Yeah, OK,' so I took him in.

RR What happened then?

AY Well, I started firing questions at him about the Bible, about how it contradicts itself – I had been thinking a long while on this – and he answered all me questions.

RR What happened then?

AY Well, at the end of the day, I finally made a commitment to Christ, and I always remember the first time I went into the Church of the Ascension. I didn't know what to expect and I was walking up and down for about half an hour and suddenly nipped in, and I didn't think anybody was watching.

RR But then the vicar landed you with quite a job. He sent you round to visit Benny didn't he?

AY He popped in one night and said, 'I've got somebody that wants to know about Jesus' and he said, 'I can't sort of get through to him, but seeing as you speak the same language as him . . .' He says, 'You probably know him – it's Benny Stafford.' And I nearly fell off me chair.

RR Why was this?

AY Well, I've known Benny all me life.

RR Benny, what were you really like beforehand?

BS Well, I think I was hard to live with. I used to sometimes, not regularly, but I've knocked Cathy, me wife, about a bit – for nothing, you know, just being drunk. I've had me share of thieving; I've been put away a couple of times – you know, been nicked, and I've had me share of drugs. I've tried everything.

**RR** What do you think really made you change?

**BS** I don't know. I now know God wanted me.

**RR** Have you got a job?

**BS** Oh yeah, I've got a beautiful job now. I look after mentally handicapped, and it's a job what I really like – really like doing. We bath them; we take them shopping; we cook for them; we take them out socially. I am sure Jesus has put me in this job. I've had offers for other jobs – more money, I might say, than what I get here – but I enjoy this job so much and I feel part of their family now.

The awayday *Songs of Praise* were that little bit different. And this is certainly true of the one that came from the Brecon Jazz Festival. I have always loved Brecon and it was good to be working again with director Dafydd Owen. He tried to persuade me to go up in a hot air balloon, but not even for *Songs of Praise* was I prepared to do that. It was another programme that went with a swing as the music was led by the Welsh National Jazz Orchestra. Everyone was in party mood but one of the interviews brought me back to reality with a bang. I went on a picnic with members of the L'Arche Community. In this community a couple of people with mental disabilities were living with a group of other young people. The leader of the group was Jim Cargin:

**RR** Jim Cargin is the Director of the local L'Arche Community which has only recently been founded on a housing estate in Brecon.

**JC** It's a place where people with a learning difficulty (and assistants) can live together and build a Christian community together. It's a place where people who might normally be marginalised at the edges of society are able to live, and live with all kinds of people, and put all our difficulties and weaknesses at the centre, and Jesus is there with it, redeeming it, transforming it and making it worthwhile. What is important is that it is not so much what we can do with our heads and our hands that is important, but what we are able to give and receive with our hearts.

So, the importance of L'Arche is that it is a place where I can discover my own dependence on God because we are a very fragile community – I mean there are just five or six of us and the boat can get rocked very easily. Which is no bad thing, because we are trying to live in the same world when everybody else's boat gets rocked as well. I don't think I could carry on living and making sense of all the boat rocking without prayer. It's not so much me speaking to God but it's God speaking to me and saying, 'Well, the boat is rocking but you're not overboard yet.' That sort of thing.

The founder of the L'Arche Community had been a guest on *Good Morning Sunday* also. What Jean Vanier had to say certainly stirred the listeners:

JV    'L'Arche' is a French word which means 'The Ark' and in our world there are a lot of people in pain, a lot of people being smothered by a world of efficacity, competition and rivalry. Amongst those people that are being stifled, smothered, pushed aside, are people who are weak, fragile, because of a mental handicap. And so that is what 'L'Arche' is about. It's an Ark where we welcome in small family homes men and women who have been pushed aside, pushed into institutions, who are living in unbearable situations because of a handicap.

RR    Now how did this idea come about?

JV    It began when I met a priest who was chaplain to a residence in France. He awoke in me the realisation that weak people were being crushed. I started to visit psychiatric hospitals, asylums, institutions and I found a vast world of oppressed, terribly suffering people. You know, on hospital wards you would find maybe sixty to a hundred people, no work, turning around in circles, obviously in a lot of inner pain. So what I did was to welcome two men who I found in an asylum – they had been put there because their parents had died, Raphael had had meningitis when he was young, Philippe had had encephalitis when he was young. They had the consequences of these two sicknesses – difficulties in speaking, walking and so on. When their parents had died they had been put into the asylum, and I asked just the two of them if they would like to come and live with me.

It was that sort of interview that helped redress the balance of any interview that might be considered lightweight or of little consequence. However, when *Good Morning Sunday* was on an awayday the emphasis was usually on fun. The first seaside resort we visited, and to which we returned because of the wonderful way we were treated by their director of tourism, was Bournemouth. At the end of the pier is a café which was just right for a broadcast. As the main guest we tried to invite someone who was appearing locally in a summer show. One of the most successful guests we invited was Roy Castle. So successful that Roy, with his wife Fiona, were our guests one Christmas Eve. Roy is very musical and backed by the group, Chicago Classic, he put heart and soul into a musical item which explained how it was possible to praise God on many instruments.

Obviously, if there was anything unique about the resort we would aim to capture that. Bournemouth has some very special illuminations; instead of the usual lights festooned along the front, Bournemouth sets aside spaces in one of its parks on the front for some very attractive displays which are lit not by electric light bulbs but by candles. One year I was there we managed to record the lighting of the candles and I talked to a young girl whose design had won a competition for pride of place in the gardens.

When it comes to illuminations, of course, the first place that comes to mind is Blackpool. One summer we headed north to Lancashire's most famous resort. Getting there had had its difficulties. The train on which we left London was not a through one so it was necessary to change at Preston. This we duly did. There wasn't a long gap between our train arriving from London and the small push-me-pull-you train leaving for Blackpool; just long enough, we thought, for Hilary to go and get something from the station buffet to sustain us for the rest of the journey. We were wrong – by the time Hilary returned the train was just leaving with the rest of the team on it. The cans of drink and the Mars bars kept Hilary fortified until the next train, which fortunately, was not too long in coming.

The site for the broadcast in Blackpool was the Sandcastle Centre – a vast leisure complex which had, amongst other things, a swimming pool heated to tropical standards. With it being Blackpool there was no worry about whether there would be any star names or not. The only difficulty was encouraging them to come to record a show at about 2 p.m. With some of them having done two shows the previous evening and with two shows to do that evening they tended to guard the day for rest and relaxation. As I mentioned before, Dana was a very willing guest but we also managed to persuade two others – singer Frank Ifield and comedian Charlie Williams.

Blackpool is also famous for its fun fair and its trams. Although the producer at the time, John Forrest, adored fun fairs he realised that they were not my forte and so I was spared the ordeal of the Big Dipper or the Giant Wheel. I think I would have been so frightened that all listeners would have heard was me either screaming or being sick. Neither of which would have been ideal for a Sunday morning breakfast. The trams, however, were a different matter. It was great fun learning to drive a Blackpool tram and incredibly safe; not just for me but also for the promenaders along the front. It is purely a matter of staying on the right rails – there could be a sermon in that.

It was important that in such a programme as *Good*

*Morning Sunday* we didn't show any bias – well at least not between Lancashire and Yorkshire. So having been to Blackpool it was important that we crossed the Pennines to Scarborough. Here, down on the seafront, we had a real party – mainly due to Bobby Ball who was doing the summer season. The liveliness that he had shown during an interview that I had with him earlier was nothing in comparison to the vitality he shows to a live audience. About a thousand people were encouraged, by him, to sing 'On Ilkley Moor Bar Tat', and believe it or not we made quite a good shot at it. His Christian faith also gave him a freedom to speak out. Armed with a copy of The Salvation Army paper, *The War Cry*, I showed him the banner headline which said ' "If you're not a Christian you're a wally," says Bobby Ball.' He readily admitted that he had said it and that he had been quoted fairly. I am sure *The War Cry* is a paper which checks its facts before it publishes a story. It was great to experience his enthusiasm although I fear lovers of the traditional Book of Common Prayer and the Authorised Version of the Bible would not be too keen on the word 'wally'.

If a thousand people turned out at Scarborough, the people of Plymouth were not quite so enthusiastic for *Good Morning Sunday*. Naturally we recorded the programme on the Hoe and so as to capture the spirit of Sir Francis Drake we persuaded one of the local bowling clubs to allow us to use their pavilion. The day was wet, dismal and cold. This, however, didn't stop the bowlers enjoying their sport. Throughout the recording the bowlers went in and out of their pavilion with little attention to what was going on. It was a matter of getting one's priorities right. However, it made life difficult for comedian/impressionist Peter Goodwright who was trying to entertain those members of the audience who were prepared to be static, well at least for a short while.

There was another visit to the coast, and this was to Yarmouth on the Isle of Wight. This was a rather special visit because it was to a holiday organised by the magazine *Woman's Realm*. For a number of years they had organised this holiday which was the brainchild of their then problem-page editor, Clare Shepherd. It was called Find a Friend and its original intention was that it should be a relaxed holiday for people after they had been widowed or divorced. The popularity of the holiday grew and it became a regular booking for many who felt at home in these sort of surroundings. Along with some of the *Woman's Realm* staff I went to spend a day or so with the holidaymakers. Monday was my regular day for being there as it was then that Clare's successor, Gill Cox, and I did a session together. We would take a subject, like prejudice, and sitting on two stools would discuss it, audience participation being encouraged. Although attendance at this session was obviously voluntary for the holidaymakers the vast majority came and what's more seemed to enjoy themselves. Those who were in the archery competition were excused. During a day of Find a Friend there was so much to do it was impossible to fit in everything.

To broadcast *Good Morning Sunday* from here was a natural. The microphones were set up in the dining room and I got on with the programme while everyone else enjoyed their breakfast. I tried to have my breakfast at the same time but my kippers took a long time to appear and were not easy to eat whilst speaking to the nation. Some of the holidaymakers found it hard to believe that the programme was going out live so often they would come up to have a chat or to ask me to sign a photograph just at the time when I was meant to be dedicating the next record.

Amongst the people I chatted to on the programme was, of course, Gill Cox:

**RR**  Gill, what do you think actually makes a friend?

**GC**  Well, I think it's easier said than done. You need to find them first of all.

**RR**  Where *do* you find them?

**GC**  Well, I recommend if people don't know where to go, I think clubs are a good place to start. There are all sorts of things, there's Women's Institute, Townswomen's Guild, evening classes – I mean all sorts of places where you will actually meet and come into contact with other people. And it's not easy. If you live in a street where, you know, there are lots of people up and down. If it's a small village you're fine – if you live in a place like London – hopeless. You might not see them from one week to the next. So I think you often need to actually go somewhere where you will meet and talk to people. That's step one.

RR  Actually I find some Churches are very friendly indeed and you can go in. I know that sometimes some people go to Church and they feel no one speaks to them, but a lot of Churches I go into people are very friendly and they welcome strangers and say hello, and that's very nice indeed.

GC  Yes, but then you need step two, don't you? You need to be able to move from that club environment, or from a Church or wherever, back to actually having people in your own home and being able to develop a friendship. That's stage two.

RR  People are very nervous about that because they feel that they're making a commitment of some sort and some people won't make a commitment in any direction. How do you overcome that?

GC  Well, I think that's difficult. You have stumped yourself before you begin. That's not to say that if you get friendly with someone and then you find out that actually they're a pain in the neck that you can't then move on from there and move into different friendships – not just dump that person, but move away again, move back again. But, you see you don't meet one person one day and become extremely firm friends the next unless you're in an environment like this, where you're all living together for a week, where firm friendships can be made in a very short space of time because you're living and breathing and enjoying things with each other.

RR  So if you're not living together, how do you make them then?

GC  Well, I think inviting people into your own home is

a good way of doing it and not necessarily the formal dinner party set-up. I mean, I find that having a cup of coffee over the kitchen table is often where friendships are made and cemented, because then you often – in that more relaxed, less formal environment you get down to the nitty-gritty really, don't you.

**RR** But what's the most vital thing about a friendship?

**GC** Well, companionship, mutual support, a sense of humour, listening to each other, understanding each other, generosity – and I don't necessarily mean generosity as in buying each other things, generosity of spirit.

**RR** I find trust is absolutely vital. I mean, if there isn't trust a friendship disintegrates, doesn't it?

**GC** Yes, if you feel that you give someone a confidence and they're immediately going to broadcast it up and down the street, well, you're not going to be that friendly with them really.

While the Find a Friend holiday was to encourage people on their own to come away on holiday, the WRVS does sterling work with those who have to stay at home. To celebrate the fiftieth anniversary of the WRVS I went up to Manchester to join a local team. One of the first jobs I determined to do was help deliver the Meals on Wheels. They made me do this thoroughly and I started at the kitchen where I saw the food prepared before heading off on a round. You can't waste time on this job for fear of the food getting cold, but neither can you be in such a rush that you have no time to talk. At some houses it can be that you are the only visitor that day. I had to learn the system of knocks or rings to gain entrance and people were always pleased to see me. One gentleman had his table properly laid waiting for the dish of the day and every single one of them had their money, and the exact money, ready. It's interesting how many of those who are housebound can be far better organised than those of us who are able to get out and about.

For those who could get out there was an afternoon club. It

was obvious that this was a regular must in many women's diaries, even if they had to cycle to get there. The atmosphere was one of happiness and friendship, all lovingly organised by those ladies in sage green. It isn't only the senior citizens and the housebound who are cared for by the WRVS. At Withington Hospital I saw a well-stocked and efficiently-run tea bar which was a great comfort especially to relatives and friends of patients who had travelled a fair distance to visit them. And at Booth Hall Children's Hospital parents of sick children were grateful for a room which the WRVS had had built on to a ward, so that those that needed to stay with their children could. One member of staff was only too pleased to express her gratitude:

**RR**     Sister French, how useful is this stay unit here?
**SF**     Very useful. We're finding that it's used every night of the week now and we haven't got enough room – we'd like more.
**RR**     How many parents can you get in here?
**SF**     We can get three in at the moment. We have two beds that have been provided and a bed-chair which is used, obviously, after the two beds are taken up.
**RR**     Now is it a help to you as a Sister in the ward to have the parents about, or are they a nightmare?
**SF**     No, they're a great help, especially in the times of hardship or shortage of nurses, then the parents do an awful lot for us.
**RR**     And what's wrong with your patients in here?
**SF**     They're all orthopedic patients – children that have broken bones, spina bifida, bone abnormalities, soft tissue abnormalities or patients with congenital dislocations of the hip.
**RR**     So they can be here quite a while?
**SF**     They can, yes.
**RR**     Do you find entertaining them a full time job?
**SF**     Definitely!

Dame Barbara Shenfield, the Head of the WRVS, made a very welcome guest appearance on the programme:

**RR**    This is your Golden Jubilee Year. How are you celebrating it?

**BS**    Well, we have had services all over the country because I think all our members felt that it was an occasion not just for jollification, but an occasion to be thankful for good work done by many of our dedicated, long-serving members and to be thankful for the good things that I think voluntary services of this kind can achieve for the community. So everywhere we have had first of all cathedral or church services, and various other kinds of celebrations. But mostly we're using it as an occasion to look back, see what lessons there are to be learnt and do a bit of stock-taking, and see what we're going to do for the future.

**RR**    Do many of the people who take part in these services, your supporters, feel that this is part of their Christian service?

**BS**    I think they do. I think all the great religions have always enjoined one to love one's neighbour, to take care of the stranger within one's gates. I think this is part of people's attitude to life, and voluntary services are a very useful channel for being able to put these feelings of wanting to help others to good effect.

**RR**    I also hear you've got a bit of glory – you've got a rose of your own.

**BS**    Oh yes, that's rather nice. Somebody has bred us a new rose called the Royal Volunteer, to be around in the autumn and we hope people will be planting it in their gardens because again it's a little commemoration. We've got a lot of them planted in Westminster Abbey gardens.

Two of the nation's patron saints were given the VIP treatment with special programmes in their honour. To commemorate St David we took the programme to my home town of Cardiff. I was able to stay with friends. For the rest of the team life wasn't quite so peaceful. They booked themselves into a hotel which, on the Saturday night, had a disco immediately below their rooms. This is no joke when you are getting up at about 5 a.m. The studios for the BBC in Wales are in Llandaff, not far from the cathedral, for which I have great affection. I also had great affection for one particular guest on the programme. Alongside our tribute to St David the producer had decided to find out a little about my childhood. So we went to Tremorfa, an area of Cardiff next door to Splott, to interview Mabel Kelly. Mabel had been a cleaner at the vicarage where I spent the first seventeen months of my life, but Mabel and her husband Tom had remained very good friends. They never forgot me at either birthdays or Christmas and Mabel was particularly faithful in her prayers at the time of the anniversaries of the deaths of my parents. I think she quite enjoyed having her little say about me:

RR     You cleaned the vicarage where I first lived, didn't you?

MK     Yes.

RR     How long – how many years did you do that?

MK     Ten years.

RR     Marvellous.

MK     From the time your dad came into the parish. I was at Evensong when he asked me would I go down.

RR     And were you there when I was born?

MK     Well, I wasn't in the house when you were born 'cos you were born in Connaught Nursing Home run by The Salvation Army.

RR     Do you know, I never knew that. Was I a good baby?

MK     Oh, yes, you were a good baby really. Only you used to shout up in the garden a lot.

RR     But you've kept the link ever since. I mean, you've written regularly and I've popped in to see you and we've phoned one another. You know, when about three years ago you came to see me at the New Theatre in pantomime . . .

MK     Yes.

RR     . . . with Ruth Madoc and Steve Francis. I mean, do

you think my parents would have approved of that?

MK    Oh I think so. Your dad had a sense of humour and your mam. I shouldn't say that. We used to clean the vicarage and then your mother would decide on the 'Beetledrive' in the lounge, and it would be all over again, cleaning it.

RR    That's not my idea of a sense of humour, to be honest. What about being a broadcaster, now I'm allowed to broadcast. Do you think they would have approved of that?

MK    Oh, I think they'd be proud of you.

St George was commemorated in that very English of places, Bath. The local branch of the Royal Society of St George made sure that we were well kitted out with roses while some Girl Guides, including a company from nearby Bradford on Avon, along with some Scouts, did their bit and turned out as dragons.

Bath is a place with a great history and I was delighted to delve into it:

RR    I've come down to the Roman Baths and I'm standing near the spring, which obviously you can hear because for the last eight thousand years it has been pumping out healthy hot mineral water at the rate of a quarter of a million gallons a day. And here to tell me more about this miracle of nature is Stephen Bird who is the Assistant Director of Roman Baths. Stephen, good morning to you.

SB    Good morning, Roger.

RR    Where is it coming from?

SB    We don't really know, the geologists are divided in their opinions but we think it falls as rainwater on the hills somewhere in the south-west of Britain and percolates its way down through the geological strata, eventually to be forced up under pressure in Bath and that cycle may take something like twenty thousand years to achieve.

RR    It's like my pipes at home, it's terrible getting the water through them. Why is it hot?

SB    It's hot because as it goes down into the earth's crust it gets heated, simply from the depth it goes to and as it is heated so it expands and that forces it up through the fissure under Bath.

RR    Is it healthy water?

SB    We know that it's very mineral-rich, there are something like forty-three different minerals in it, and so drinking it certainly has always been beneficial to people. Whether taking it externally, though, that is swimming in it, is beneficial is less certain.

RR    But it's been like a sauna, hasn't it?

SB    Oh indeed, yes. Bath has been a spa for the last two thousand years, on and off. The Romans built a magnificent curative complex and religious complex around this hot spring where the pilgrims came perhaps to seek healing in the hot water.

As well as being St George's Day it was also the start of Radio 2's Health Check Fortnight and so I was able to talk to diet writer Dr Barry Lynch. But the thought of diet didn't put me off my stride when it came to tackling the world-famous bun. I sampled this culinary delight at Sally Lunn's where I chatted to Mike Overton:

RR    Now the Sally Bun, Mike, is this the same as a Bath Bun?

MO    No, no, they are different, and it's basically a very rich bread made with eggs and butter.

RR    It's a bread, rather than a bun?

MO    That's right.

RR    May I just try it.

MO    I hope you will, and I hope you enjoy it.

RR    It looks enormous . . . it's very nice.

MO    It is indeed, isn't it?

RR    It's got a tiny touch of the Hot Cross Bun about it, but without the spicy bit.

**MO**    No, no spices, but the richness, yes.

**RR**    I'm making a heck of mess, I'm sorry – look at all these crumbs.

**MO**    That's why Esther brought you a knife and fork.

**RR**    If only I had done what she said I would have been perfectly all right. Any chance of having the recipe?

**MO**    Not a chance.

**RR**    Now, why not?

**MO**    Because it's part of the heritage of Bath and it's part of the heritage of this house, and I have sworn to keep it secret and pass it on when my time comes to go.

**RR**    Fair enough.

There was one place well off the beaten track that we visited one Harvest. It is a community in the heart of the Dorset countryside, in the tiny hamlet of Pilsdon. The priest who led it, Stuart Affleck, was well known to me since he had been chaplain at Charterhouse when I was chaplain at Eton. I had also visited the community on many occasions and have tremendous respect for the work it does. There are times in many people's lives when things can get the better of them and everything becomes that little bit too much. Pilsdon is there to help you get things back into perspective again. At its heart is a chapel and a life of prayer, but the day to day round of tending the garden, growing the vegetables, caring for the animals, are also a vital part of its daily life. What impressed me most about the community was the way in which Stuart would greet everyone at meal times. You don't just walk into the dining room and look for somewhere to sit hoping that someone will talk to you. Everyone is ushered to a seat so that there can be no set places and those who have arrived for their first meal feel just as much at home as those who have been in the community for a long time.

As many churches treat Harvest seriously, so did we. As well as a visit to Pilsdon we also visited a lovely farm at Harescombe in Gloucestershire where the farmer and his wife couldn't have made us more welcome. The only sad memory of that particular broadcast was that it was the last time I worked with Ted Moult.

Our visit to Bradford might have surprised a few people. The cathedral was staging a special Wool Festival and I did the programme from the Dean's House. There was one problem. On the Green outside the cathedral were some sheep, but they were silent sheep. On television they would have looked lovely but on radio there was something lacking. I felt a little better when the shepherd, who came with them, said that they only made a noise when they were nervous and as we tried to relax all our guests on *Good Morning Sunday* I was glad that the sheep felt included.

Handsworth, in Birmingham, was also visited as an away-day. The choir of the New Testament Church of God had won an award and so we thought we would share in their celebrations. It was good to be able to present the positive side of an area which had seen difficulties. The singing was very infectious and it was impossible, that morning, to doze off once you'd switched on. I also remember, after the broadcast, being supplied with a very healthy breakfast.

Often we were spoiled on our outside broadcasts and on the door of the *Good Morning Sunday* office there is living proof of the generosity of some of the people we visited. Frank Howard, who we met when we went to East Devon for a programme that highlighted the life of the local bellringing community, gave us a wonderful carving representing *Good Morning Sunday*. It now greets those who cross the threshold into the world of *Good Morning Sunday*.

# AN INNOCENT ABROAD

If you want people to be 'up-front' about their religion there is only one place to go and that's the United States of America. Whereas with British guests I had sometimes to find a subtle way of establishing whether they had any faith at all, with Americans it was often just a matter of pressing the right button and I got the answers I needed.

The only way to get American guests en masse was to go to the States and meet them on their home ground. As I mentioned before, this was easier said than done. Before we left on any American tour a tremendous amount of preparatory work had to be done by the researchers. Because of the time gap this meant late-night phoning and often it would take many calls to get one guest as agents had a habit of stringing us along.

The Angel Awards being held in Los Angeles was one time when we knew that we would be able to get a certain number of American guests together. These awards, which were seen by some as the 'religious Oscars' (although the competition was nowhere near so intense) were the dreamchild of Mary Dore, who had the backing of the then President, Ronald Reagan, for her ambitious scheme. On the night I took part in the award ceremony and actually received an award, the event was held in the Coconut Grove on Wilshire Boulevard. Laser beams played on the front of the hotel, people dressed as robotic angels greeted us in the foyer, and where the presentations took place Hollywood's razzmatazz was well to the fore.

One of my co-presenters at the ceremony was the actress Susan Howard, who was appearing in *Dynasty*. On my first visit to the USA we had been unable to find a suitable time to meet but when I went back later I managed to meet her and her husband in a hotel in Los Angeles. It was a very worthwhile meeting. She is a very committed Christian and she told me of some of the challenges that face a Christian in a 'soap', which seemed to reflect little of Christian values:

RR    Susan, we were talking about the demands that are put on a Christian. You have had to face these with scripts that you've had for instance, in *Dallas* and the possibility of an abortion. Now how did you face that?

SH    Well because God's very wise and very kind. He gives you ways to deal with things. In *Dallas* Steve and I over the years had said, 'Why don't we have a baby, I mean, good grief, everybody on this show has a baby, but Ray and Donna! And everybody keeps telling us we should have a baby.' And they said, 'OK, OK, OK, you can have a baby.' So they built Ray and Donna a bedroom and Donna got pregnant. Then they came to me at the end of the year and said, 'We decided that Donna is going to have an abortion next year' and my heart really sunk to the floor. I said, 'Well, wait a minute, why?' and they said, 'Well, because she is going to discover that she is carrying a Down's syndrome child.' 'Well, what does that have to do with it?' I asked and they said, 'Well, 98 per cent of the people who find out they're carrying a Down's syndrome child choose abortion.' I said, 'Well, what about the other 2 per cent?' and they replied, 'Well, I guess they must want it.' I argued, 'Don't you think Donna's character – the way that she has been over these past years, and they have waited all this time – that she would think "I can deal with this, I can handle this"?' They said, 'No, no, no, no, no.'

So we got into a whole thing about it and I said to

them, 'You know, on this show, you, the networks, CBS, Lorimar, everybody involved keeps telling us that what you want to do is present a balance. You want to always show both sides of everything. You are yet to do that, because what you have done in the seven years that we have been on the air is, you've had two abortions by two major characters on the show, and never once did you ever discuss the possibility of those people choosing life over death.' And I said, 'We need to deal with this. You need to show someone choosing life.' In the midst of this, while they were totally opposed to it, a gentleman named Phil Capese, really rallied behind me. Phil at that time was the executive producer of the show, and he asked me a very difficult question: 'At this point of time in your life, Susan, if you found that you were pregnant, you were carrying a Down's syndrome child, what would you do?' It's not an easy thing to say, Roger, because there would have been a time in my life before I came to know what life was that I would have not even given it a thought, because we live in a world that says we want things to be perfect and whole . . .

RR     . . . and convenient.

SH     . . . and convenient. And if it, in any way displeasures me or causes me any kind of complication, let's just dispose of it, and I said to him, 'Phil, with all my heart, I would have that child.' And he said, 'OK, I will take care of it. Donna will not have an abortion.'

Charlene Tilton is another lady who is both a Christian and knows what life is like for an actress in a television soap. She is petite, but her views are not, especially when it comes to her belief:

RR     Religion is very much an important part of your present marriage, isn't it?

*127*

CT      Religion is not necessarily an important part of my life, because I was brought up and I know a lot of people were brought up with this strict confinement of religiosity. No, that to me is not important. What is important is the Word of God – I believe that the Bible is the inspired Word of God, and that Jesus Christ over two thousand years ago came and died on the Cross to save our sins. But I do not believe in religiosity, about lighting the candles and eating your fish on Friday, and . . .

RR      So the petty rules mean nothing?

CT      No, they don't. What means something to me, is keeping an open heart before the Lord and giving Him place in your life to touch other people.

RR      What brought about this longing for faith?

CT      Well, to put it in a nutshell . . . I just knew that there was a void in my life. All the money in the world can't buy it, all the relationships in the world can't buy it, all the friends. There was just a void, that *is* there until it is filled.

I visited Charlene in her very beautiful Californian home with her husband and daughter. It wasn't possible to meet all the stars in such relaxing surroundings. Amy Grant is a singer whose records featured frequently on the show. She was a natural for an interview. She was not at home, being on tour with her Christian rock show but we managed to catch up with her in Fort Smith in Arkansas. The concert was being held in a cattle market. Now my idea of a concert is in a hall, like the Royal Festival Hall or the St David's Hall in Cardiff. My way of thinking says cattle markets are for cattle. I interviewed Amy in her caravan before the concert took place, a caravan that was in no way short of this world's comforts. Since she had been so generous with her time for the interview, the team felt it only right to attend her concert. A mighty stage had been erected, batteries of lights had been put into place and, that essential of any rock show, Christian or otherwise, the loudspeakers, had been sited. Hilary, the producer and Bobbette the researcher fitted comfortably into the surroundings both knowing the rock world and both nearer the age range of the audience than I. At fifty I certainly stretched that age range by more than a decade or two. I didn't manage the whole concert, though considering my age and my condition thought I did pretty well.

Amy may be a belter on stage but she had serious things to say about the life she leads face to face:

RR    Amy, you're doing a great sort of mixture these days, between your Christian singing and what might be termed your pop or secular singing. Do you find any difficulties bridging the two?

AG    No, not really. I mean, I have to assume that the people that listen to my music surely have common experiences with me, and the songs that I write are just about life, either as I've experienced it or as I've seen other people experience it. And, if anything, I think that there can be a pitfall for people in the public eye, just portraying one facet of who they are. And, I mean, goodness knows, everybody wants to put their best foot forward, but if you keep sticking that best foot forward and you don't catch the other one up, you know, you're going to fall flat on your face.

RR    So you don't always want to be a sort of preacher woman through your music?

AG    Oh, no. Especially, I think, for the audience that I want to sing to, which is primarily young. I don't think it's the quantity of information these kids are hit with, I think it's a timely word spoken. It's the quality of what is said. A lot of times the songs I write aren't specifically Christian songs, they're just relationship songs, or maybe, experiences that I've had and, hopefully, they're building a foundation of a relationship for me to eventually come in and say, 'Well, let me tell you something about my faith.'

If Charlene and, to a certain extent, Amy are considered to

be on the petite side, one American guest that I had on the programme was not. Richard Keil, who played Jaws in the Bond movies, is 7'2″. When I visited him in his home he was minus the steel teeth that he used for the part, but his height was all him. I have a photograph of myself taken with Richard and I look like a cardboard cutout alongside his great height. But Richard's head was not in the clouds when it came to coping with his own life:

**RR**    You felt you wanted healing in your own life, why?

**RK**    Well, I had a problem with alcohol and it got to the point where I was putting vodka into my beer and wine to make it stronger and putting scotch into my coffee in the morning.

**RR**    Makes it stand up, doesn't it?

**RK**    Oh, (laughs) makes you default out, but that was about nine and a half years ago and I was quite worried about it, and ashamed, but I was addicted to the alcohol like people get addicted to cigarettes and some people, drugs. And I couldn't shake it, I tried, in fact, I made a film in Yugoslavia with a very fine British actor who had a similar problem and I saw that man – shortly afterwards he died – and he had quite a number of children and a little infant baby. I had three children and another one coming and I knew that I had to do something. And I was watching television, Christian television, one morning and a man invited Christians to accept Christ and be free of these types of things, but he also went one step further and suggested that Christians who had accepted Jesus when they were young who were experiencing any kind of problems or bondage, whether it's cigarettes or alcohol or whatever, that we could pray together and actually bind this thing on earth in agreement through the name of Jesus. And you know there's a scripture that says that we don't have to live in a spirit of fear, as adopted sons and daughters . . .

**RR**    Perfect love casts out fear.

RK      . . . that we have the right to cry out 'Abba', 'Daddy', 'Papa' for help. So that's what I did that morning and God just totally took away all addiction for alcohol I had. I am not an alcoholic any more and I'm no longer addicted to it.

RR      And how has that changed your thinking about Jesus?

RK      Well, it makes me realise the power of Jesus' name; and the fact that God is alive and real, and you know, he's been real in my life.

Richard had thought deeply about his faith. It was good for me to be able to see the other side of someone whom I'd previously thought of as a fairly violent character.

If you are looking for violence you need look no further than the television programme, *The A Team*. Although right always prevails in this programme the way in which it is achieved leaves a fair bit to be desired. The character who must have achieved more notoriety than any other person in the series is Mr T. Mr T is not a person to be trifled with in his screen persona, nor is he to be taken lightly in real life.

Before I was allowed to interview him I had to watch an episode of this television series being filmed. This was quite useful as it gave me some extra background information. Instead of settling down to do the interview when the filming stopped, Mr T went to meet a family. At first I was rather annoyed; then I learned that a child of the family was dying and it had been his wish to meet Mr T. From the look in the child's eyes this dream had more than met expectation. When Mr T had finished talking to the family and showing them round the set, I got ready once again to do the interview. Yet again I was thwarted as Mr T headed for his caravan. It was obvious that he didn't want to be disturbed. Eventually the interview took place on the way from his caravan to his car. The circumstances weren't ideal and I still don't know the man behind the mask.

No mask was needed by one guest who I'd looked forward to meeting and who fulfilled expectations. For years I have enjoyed the singing of Dionne Warwick and got the opportunity to interview her while she was in cabaret at Caesar's Palace in Las Vegas. An earlier visit to the States had taken me to Reno to meet singing star Glen Campbell so I had some idea of what a gambling town was like. Las Vegas was Reno, but bigger and glitzier. At night the neon signs light up the sky. When day dawns the town resembles the desert from whence it came, though the desert is more beautiful.

The single aim of Las Vegas is to get people gambling. As soon as you enter any hotel you are confronted by machines with people sitting by them holding cardboard buckets containing tokens with which to feed the greedy beasts. The humans appear to be transfixed, mesmerised, hoping against hope that luck will 'be a lady tonight'. As you get further into the hotels so you come across the more serious gamblers, playing various games at tables, watched over by people who have but one interest and that is to see that the rules of the house are obeyed.

Amidst this rather depressing scene are restaurants serving food at very reasonable prices and a theatre, where on stage each night there is a star attraction. Dionne Warwick filled that role with ease while I was there and kindly agreed to be interviewed in her suite in the hotel. The suite seemed bigger than many people's homes but she couldn't have been more welcoming and it was interesting to hear about her musical and religious beginnings:

RR  Now, when was it discovered you had got such a super voice?

DW  Well thank you first of all for the compliment. I've been singing since I was six years old and it started in my grandpa's Church – he kind of stood me up on a chair behind his podium to sing 'Amazing Grace', which was one of his favourite songs, and I guess that's where it all started.

RR  Was your grandpa a preacher?

DW  Yes, he was.

RR  What sort of Church was this, Dionne?

DW  AME – American/African Methodist Episcopal.

**RR**    Oh gosh, what a good mixture – sounds like a right cocktail. So what would have gone on in that Church? Would it have been full of music?

**DW**    Absolutely. My entire family, my mum and my dad, my aunts and uncles, my sister, we were all part of the choir, and part of the ministry, actually on the Deacon board, and Sunday School teachers. We were very, very much involved with our church activities.

**RR**    When you said you were part of the choir, a lot of the black choirs in Britain now dress beautifully when they're singing. Would this have been part of your routine?

**DW**    Yes, we had choir robes.

**RR**    And did you enjoy the performing element of that?

**DW**    Well, we didn't consider it performing. We considered it a part of our life. There's a difference between gospel music, and the performing end of it which is when you're selling something. I don't think you have to really sell God – that's my feeling anyway, and that happens to be the feeling of the entire congregation.

**RR**    Do you feel that that has stood you in good stead since leaving home and travelling the world?

**DW**    It was a very firm foundation in the world of music, in portraying the true value of a lyric. When you sing gospel music you're singing about something you truly believe in and that happens to be God. It's bringing the message through song, and it has given me that wherewithal with which to convey the message on the pop idiom, the lyric that is written, the message that is to be given, and I think my training was very sound.

In cabaret with Dionne at Caesar's Palace was Natalie Cole, the singer and daughter of Nat King Cole. Dionne and Natalie worked well together, complementing, rather than competing with each other. As part of their finale they did a very moving sequence with the recorded voice of Nat King

Cole while photographs of the Cole family were projected on to the screen.

While I was in Las Vegas on that occasion I was unable to interview Natalie, but I was fortunate enough to catch up with her one day when she was passing through London. We talked about her faith:

NC      It was through my husband as well as a member of my family that I changed my religion – I was brought up Episcopalian and I changed to Baptist, not quite a year before I actually recorded my first album. And it has changed my life significantly, being a Christian and being a Baptist.

RR      In what sort of ways?

NC      Well, I look to a different source now for my happiness, rather than looking to people and outside things, I gain my confidence and my strength from God and from myself, and we work together. It's a very nice feeling, and also I see God in other people.

RR      And do you feel God is with you when you're performing?

NC      Oh yes, I think a lot of people don't necessarily know what it is that attracts them to my performances other than a feeling, and it's more than just a personality or . . .

RR      Oh, you have a tremendous warmth for your audience.

NC      Yes, it's an energy.

RR      It's fantastic.

NC      I depend on that, you know. Most of the members of my group are Christians; it's just something that is really at the top of my life and my everyday comings and goings.

As I've said, Americans are usually up-front about their faith, but we did some interviews with people for whom faith did not appear to play an important part in life. We interviewed Ed Asner, the actor who played the part of Lou

Grant in the series of the same name. The notes we had had about him reading the Scriptures in the Synagogue on special occasions appeared to have little or no foundation. Despite his being politically active, organised religion seems to hold little for him:

**RR** How faithful have you stayed to your Jewish faith?

**EA** I fled from it as often as I could as a kid, because I was very often a single minority . . .

**RR** And did you resent that?

**EA** I resented it. I went to Hebrew school after school every day 'til I was barmitzvahed.

**RR** And I hear your barmitzvah was not a success.

**EA** You're absolutely right.

**RR** Why wasn't it a success?

**EA** I was nervous. I was doing a much bigger singing and reading job than any kid before me. The honour frightened the hell out of me. The rabbi had been on vacation and I had what I thought to be a very short period to master it all, and I was very nervous about it.

**RR** And yet you were a performer then, weren't you, because didn't you make quite a big noise in synagogues?

**EA** I always loved to get up and freewheel in terms of singing the religious songs and being cast in the playlets that we did, but this was me, solo, alone. And I tended to bomb.

**RR** Why haven't you stayed faithful?

**EA** Well, I belong to the generation where so many American boys drifted from the faith. I don't mean forgot it, although plenty did that but certainly they did not remain as religious as their fathers. There is now a resurgence of that in this country, of re-discovering, as there is with most religions. The wave of fundamentalism that has spread over the world in all religions, certainly has occurred in Judaism.

**RR** Does fundamentalism worry you?

**EA**   Very much, very much.

**RR**   Why?

**EA**   I believe in one world, first of all. One world
celebrating many different peoples, many different
types and justice for all, freedom for all. Fundamentalism creates a segregation that very often,
if it finds itself in a position of power – well let's say
Iran versus the Bahai – becomes oppressive,
repressive. In certain instances the fundamental-
ists in Israel are, I daresay, providing as much
irritation and aggravation in the relationship of
Israeli vis-à-vis Palestinian as anybody.

At the time of our visit to the States the world of the
television evangelist was in disarray. People had become
disillusioned by some of those who for many years had
professed their faith with sincerity and in the most public
manner. For me it was good to catch up with someone whose
faith was, without doubt, sincere but proclaimed through his
music and the life that he lived in the small Franciscan
community in Eureka Springs in Arkansas. John Michael
Talbot was, like Amy Grant, known to listeners of *Good
Morning Sunday* through his music, but we knew little of him
as a person. Eureka Springs is very beautiful and something
of a tourist attraction. Apart from its beauty it has another
claim to fame. Every year it stages, in the summer months, a
Passion Play, rather like Oberammergau. Eureka Springs
was never spared from plague, nor does it suffer the same
rituals and conditions that go with the Oberammergau
production. It appears to make more use of special effects.
I'm told that Jesus' ascension back into heaven leaves little to
the imagination.

Just outside this rather quaint place is the community
where John Michael Talbot lives. It is in beautiful countryside
set amongst the Ozark Mountains. The journey to the
community was way off the beaten track, demanding good
map-reading skills. At one stage I found that I'd taken the
wrong turning and travelled a few miles through Mississippi
but in the end the tortuous journey proved worthwhile:

**RR**    Tell me about the community that you live in here, John Michael.

**JM**    Well, we are what's called an integrated monastic community. We're made up of a group of single, celebate brothers and sisters and then married couples as well, so there's three categories: single, celebate and married, who live in the monastic expression. And then the non-monastic expression is called our domestic community, or we also call them 'the little brothers and sisters', and they live in their own homes and most of them live in the United States, but we have some who live around the world.

**RR**    But you came here on your own, wanting to start a Franciscan way of life.

**JM**    I came here under the inspiration of Saint Francis, only to live by myself and what essentially happened is people came and began knocking on my hermitage door. They were all kinds of folks, Catholic, non-Catholic, some were single who wanted to get married, some were celebate and wanted to enter into a religious life and remain so, and there were others who were already married.

**RR**    And was that accepted by the Church?

**JM**    Yes, it was.

**RR**    And this was the Roman Catholic Church?

**JM**    Yes, in the Roman Catholic Church we have found great support for these integrations. For one thing, there is a historical precedent, and that is the Celtic Monastic communities – Saint Hilda of Whitby, for instance, was very very famous. They were integrated communities where they had a community of monks, a community of nuns and a community of families and they were all within one monastic village. So using that historical precedent among a few others we have been able to get quite a bit of support from the Church.

One American guest I visited twice, Coretta Scott King,

the widow of the Civil Rights Leader, Martin Luther King. I first met her when she spoke at a dinner in New Jersey in memory of her husband. The second time was in her home town of Atlanta. We had gone to Atlanta because it was the twentieth anniversary of the assassination of Martin Luther King to record a special programme for Easter. Sadly, despite all the ingredients it didn't quite work as a programme.

The previous Palm Sunday morning, after I'd been to a quiet eight o'clock Holy Communion in the Episcopalian Church on Peach Tree Avenue, I went with the rest of the team to the Ebenezer Baptist Church to the main morning service. This is the Church where Martin Luther King preached for many years. One of King's daughters was sharing in the worship on this particular Sunday.

Later, as we sat in the family home, the sister of Martin, Mrs Christine King-Farris, told me about her brother:

RR      Now I don't normally give an address when I'm giving a dedication on *Good Morning Sunday*, well at least not a full one, but today I'm going to do so, because the address is 501 Auburn Avenue, Atlanta, Georgia and that's the address of the birthplace of Martin Luther King Jr and of my guest with me this morning, Mrs Christine King-Farris, his sister. A very happy Easter to you.

CK-F    Thank you.

RR      This is a lovely home. You have many visitors coming round now.

CK-F    Yes, we have visitors who come from all over the world.

RR      I notice in fact in the corner of the parlour here a piano and on it the Sunday School Hymns No. 1. Did you often sing hymns together as a family?

CK-F    Yes, my mother was a musician and each of us had to take music lessons. That is the original piano there on which we took the piano lessons, and Martin had lots of potential in playing. He learned a few majors of 'Moonlight Sonata'. So, often, when he was in company, and this was even when he was growing up and in his later years, he'd start off with the majors of 'Moonlight Sonata' and everybody would think he was such a great accomplished musician and, of course, when he got to a certain place he would just stop. Everyone thought he was a musician.

**RR** Was it always known that Martin Luther King Jr would follow in the footsteps of his father and be a minister?

**CK-F** Not always. When he was growing up there was not much indication that he would be a minister. As a matter of fact, when he went into college he said he was going to study medicine and become a doctor, but of course that soon passed away. I think that it is a tribute to my father that both my brothers followed in his footsteps, and I think it was there all the time. Perhaps they might have been fighting it, so to speak, but they had typical lives and, of course, they sat under my father and a number of other outstanding ministers so perhaps it just grew naturally.

**RR** As we come now to the twentieth anniversary of his assassination, is there any special memory of Martin Luther King that you have, as his sister?

**CK-F** Well, the special memory I have is of how dedicated he was to his calling and how he was able to let God use him in a special way. And each time I think of him and his life, I am more determined to try to do all that I can to perpetuate his legacy. He was very sincere in what he was doing to effect social change non-violently in this country.

Just down the street from the family home stands the King Center. It's a magnificent building kept very much alive by the hundreds of people who visit it each year and reflect that if the human race is to survive there needs to be racial harmony. It was at the Center that I talked to Coretta Scott King:

**RR** What would you now say was your message to the young people of America? To all America?

**CS-K**    There is a blueprint that Martin Luther King Jr has left us, for us to follow, that we have to become better informed and understand better what Martin Luther King Jr taught by reading his writings, his books and his speeches and sermons and listening to him on tape and in video and in film, and then to prepare ourselves, in a personal way, because non-violence does deal with the transformation of the individual as well as in a collective sense, working to bring about change in this society. And when we understand the Kingian philosophy, principles and strategies, and apply them, it empowers us in such a way that we can be change-agents, that will bring about effective change in this society.

**RR**    May I ask you just one last personal question, because very many of the people listening to this programme are widows. You have been a widow for twenty years now, what has sustained you through that time?

**CS-K**    I suppose it's my own faith and commitment to bringing about change in a non-violent, positive, peaceful way. I have tried to understand non-violence and to live by it, but first of all I have tried to be a good Christian; as I am a Christian and Baptist and it doesn't matter what your particular denomination is. I am encouraged because I've seen change take place and I am going to continue to be hopeful and I continue to believe that God works through people, and that if I allow myself to be that instrument of his will, that he will use me in an effective way to help in the process of creating the beloved community.

Before the team left America on that visit we had one further call to make. It was to interview someone British who had taken America, or at least Broadway, by storm. Andrew Lloyd Webber's musical, *Phantom of the Opera*, was playing to packed houses and the star attracting them was Michael

Crawford. Very kindly he not only got us seats for the show, but also gave us an interview in his dressing room. Many hours before the curtain goes up Michael arrives at the theatre in order to apply his incredible make-up.

Michael is not only a fine actor, he is a daredevil, doing a lot of his own stunts. Even performing in *Phantom* puts him to extreme physical tests. I asked him about his attitude to leading such a physically precarious life:

RR    Were you a kind of stunt child?

MC    Yes, I suppose I was. I never had any skin on my knees.

RR    Didn't this terrify your mother. I mean, I know that your father had died before you were born, but didn't it frighten your mother out of her wits?

MC    Yes it did. I don't think she sort of just let me get on with it, but she was somehow of the same way of thinking as I was, at that time. It was wonderful to have a mother like that, that you could, you know, you could go off. She was most probably glad to get me out of the house, I was such a problem in it.

RR    But what about pain. I mean, you were doing *Phantom* at the time when you had the operation for, a double hernia?

MC    It's not a lifting illness, or injury. This is to do with singing, so it's up high in the chest.

RR    Ah.

MC    This was caused through singing and through the expansion of the diaphragm. I opened up too much and so upper stomach sort of popped through. And a lot of people have got this. But anyway, in answer to your question, going back to work when I was ill was really quite necessary at the time, because Steve Barton who was my understudy and went on for me the day I was taken into hospital, fell down the trap door and twisted his knee. So therefore he played that performance with a walking stick and he was advised to take it very easy because he would be doing more damage while they got another understudy ready. So they told me this story in hospital on a Wednesday morning, and I said – I got straight out of bed, and went into the theatre – and said, 'I'll do the two shows' because I knew it would hurt me but it wouldn't be lasting damage to me whereas if he had gone on there with that knee condition as a dancer he could have maybe . . .

**RR**   Completely ruined himself, yes.

**MC**   . . . done permanent damage, yes.

When I asked him about his faith he exhibited a side of his character which is both quiet and reflective:

**RR**   Do you also get strength from a spiritual dimension? I know, at least, in one of the papers I read about you, that prayer is something that is important to you. Do you find that you get strength from that? And what, in fact, does religion mean to you?

**MC**   That's just a very personal thing, and it's private. I do get a lot of strength. I believe and that's it. I just have my own sort of communication.

Visits to America were always worthwhile, however demanding. There was always a tremendous amount of travelling to be done. Airport lounges lose their attraction after a while and waiting for buses to take you to hire car pick-up places can seem to be a very tedious exercise. The value was the realisation that each interview added another dimension to the programme and helped to put the listeners in mind of the worldwide quality of the Christian faith.

# THROUGH SUFFERING TO STRENGTH

It is quite true that people seem to be far more interested in bad news than they are in good. They will sit gripped while someone tells them about the suffering they have undergone, while the moment someone tells them about their successes they think they are boasting and quickly turn off. Real suffering, however, tends to be far more private and getting people to talk about the experiences that they have endured is not easy. Fortunately, for Christians, there lies at the heart of the Gospel story the example of supreme suffering and what is more it is suffering that is overcome. It is this theme of overcoming suffering and disabilities which lies at the heart of many of the *Songs of Praise* interviews. I so respected the people who were willing to share their experiences in this way and, like many others, I learnt a lot from them.

There was a time when I frequently visited Northern Ireland for *Songs of Praise* and I very much enjoyed working with Jim Skelly and his team. The people of Northern Ireland must be amongst the most hospitable people in the United Kingdom. They are also generous in their openness. All programmes in the Province were ecumenical and acted as a balance to the news of division and bitterness with which we were generally fed. However, it was not possible to record programmes without some reference to the religious divide. Several of the guests had suffered because of it:

**RR**     Martine Playford grew up in this small Roman

Catholic community, St Matthew's, in East Belfast.

**MP** My job is secretary to Father O'Brien, Parish Priest. He wants to create a better place for the people of the Short Strand. He wants to open doors for the people of St Matthew's and in that way I help by assessing them, meetings with Government agents and also the Belfast Education Levy Board to get sponsorship for facilities for the area.

**RR** Martine, as a Roman Catholic, you were born and you have grown up in this area. Did you find it difficult?

**MP** Well, my sister was shot in the early seventies and we were ambushed out of our home just at the bottom of Bryston Street, and we had to move closer to the Police Station.

**RR** Would you have moved out altogether, and do you in fact think that the Catholics should move out?

**MP** No, because I think there is hope for the people of the Short Strand to mix with Protestants in the area itself.

**RR** Do you feel less embarrassed socialising with Protestants now?

**MP** No. I have never felt embarrassed socialising with Protestants because I have grown up with Protestants and mixed with them all my life. But now I think there is hope for the people of St Matthew's that they won't feel frightened of walking with a Protestant or speaking to a Protestant when they are passing other people.

**RR** And what about the Protestants' attitude towards the Catholics? Do you think that has changed?

**MP** Well, I would like to think that the Protestants would like to socialise as much with the Catholics as the Catholics would with each other. Instead of fighting against each other, I think they should be united with each other.

**RR** Martine, you are a young person in this area – now

a lot of people have given up their faith, but you haven't. Why?

**MP** Because I think faith is a very strong thing which you need throughout everyday life. If you don't have faith, you won't have confidence in yourself and also you won't have the feeling that if ever you are in trouble or you are ever in need that you can always turn to God. I never turn to him when I *need* something. It's in everyday life I speak to God and I have faith in Him.

In one programme from Scotland I witnessed the ability of men and women to overcome suffering and not only in the interviews. I had gone to Falkirk to record what probably was, for me, my most memorable *Songs of Praise*. The congregation consisted of both hearing people and people with hearing difficulties, some of whom were profoundly deaf. People had travelled from all over Scotland and some had even come from as far north as Elgin to take part in the recording. It was an extremely cold night and the recording was not made any easier by the decision of one of the cameras to play up. With television there is so much more that can go wrong than there is with radio, and you soon realise how dependent you are on machines. Not an easy lesson for me because I don't understand machines and I get very impatient with them. It meant that the recording took longer than expected but this in no way dampened the spirits of the congregation. We used the time to learn sign language. Throughout the programme signing was used so that those with hearing difficulties would be able to understand and enjoy what was being said. To help the people appreciate the hymns, not only were they sung but they were also interpreted (if that is the right word) by a signing choir. This was something I had never experienced before. It both added to the understanding of the hymns and was also pleasing to watch, rather like a manual version of formation dancing, or synchronised swimming.

It was, however, during the interviews that I really understood the courage and the faith of the people. The

Albany Church in Edinburgh was the first Church to meet both the spiritual and social needs of the deaf, and from here the mission spread worldwide.

I talked to Maisie Bailey, one of the Elders of the Church, and her Minister, Malcolm Roux, interpreted for me:

**MB**    When the deaf go to a hearing people's Church the Minister preaches and talks and talks and talks but the deaf people can't follow what the Minister is preaching about. Also with the singing and the praying the deaf people have to wait there peacefully in silence and watch their watches going round, whereas the hearing are listening to all this. The deaf, they feel just left out. It's not good really for deaf people in a hearing Church.

**RR**    You have been denied the gift of hearing. Do you think you have been given other gifts to compensate?

**MB**    I think God has given me gifts of the hands. It's wonderful what deaf people can communicate with their hands – it's absolutely wonderful and they have a lot of gifts from God. God has given deaf people work to do, just the same as hearing people. It's the same with blind people and deaf people and blind/deaf people – they can even spell on their hands. It's wonderful what we can do. God has given us a lot of truth inside ourselves. God asked me to go and see my friend who is deaf and blind, and help her to be happy and have more interests in life.

Evelyn Glennie is one of Britain's top young percussionists and she is also deaf.

**EG**    I can spend anything up to a year learning one piece. If it's a fairly large piece of music then I like to have plenty of time so that I can learn the orchestral parts as well as my own part. We always make sure there is plenty of communication, facial communication. If I am playing with a pianist I make sure I can see inside the grand piano, the foot pedal, the face, the keyboard and so on, and so really there have never been any problems.

**RR**  Do you also try and feel the music?

**EG**  I feel the actual vibrations – for example, with the low sounds of the timpani or bass drum or something like that. I can detect which range, or which note range rather, I'm playing, and it's much harder with the higher range because sometimes I can feel it in my cheek bones or hair, wherever, and I know it's a very high sound, but the lower sounds are much easier actually to detect which note or range of notes are being played.

**RR**  You obviously have a lot of courage and determination. Do you also have a faith?

**EG**  I went through a stage where I almost forgot about God in a way and only now, over the past few years, have I had time to be on my own and to think for myself what I want, what's around me and so on, and I have very much gone back to him, and so I have a lot of faith and it just, you know, gives me great oomph to face every day.

Blindness is another disability through which many people travel. This was brought home to me during a visit to a college for the blind in Worcester. I had gone to interview one of the teachers but while we were there we filmed choir practice. As one of the blind students sang 'In the Bleak Mid-Winter' I watched with tears in my eyes. I don't know why I was crying because the students showed no signs of self pity. It was just that I was so moved, not only by the quality of the singing but also by the way in which the youngsters cared for one another, especially when the huge braille music books got into undiluted confusion.

A blind person, whom I interviewed on *Good Morning Sunday*, certainly sought no pity whatsoever. Marilyn Baker claimed her ability to cope stemmed from the sustained help that she received both from her friends and especially from her faith:

**RR** So at what stage in your life did you become a Christian?

**MB** When I was a teenager at boarding school. It was through meeting a Christian family that used to take me out on a Sunday, because we loved going out to people's homes, you know, and I'd always have tea with them.

**RR** That used to happen to me when I was at school as well.

**MB** Was it? Yes, well, the way to your heart isn't it, your stomach. It is to mine! And I certainly saw a difference in these people, and they took me along to their Church, and instead of just being boring, slow hymns and things, you know, that never seemed to be very relevant, these people were obviously talking to a God that was real to them.

**RR** And what do you feel that you're offering now, through your Christian music?

**MB** Well, I feel that, hopefully, I'm speaking to people who are just ordinary people – they don't necessarily know, sort of, churchey language, but they want to know that they're important to somebody and that somebody is God, because human beings, you know, they come and go, don't they. Relationships don't last, unfortunately, death and things take them away from us, but the relationship that's permanent and secure is his relationship with us and we can all enter into it – no one's an exception to that.

**RR** One death that meant a tremendous amount to you, of course, was the death of your mother . . .

**MB** Yes.

**RR** . . . who died of leukaemia. How did you actually cope with that?

**MB** I found it difficult. I couldn't bear to see her suffering. I felt physically very ill and drained. I think we all did. But, yet, I know that at the end, especially, she came to that personal relationship with Jesus, herself. And I know that although she's died peacefully, you know, she's not really dead. I said to her, actually at her death, 'It's not goodbye, mum, it's just goodbye for a bit and that's a wonderful hope.'

RR  Do you ever feel resentful that she's not near you these days?

MB  Not resentful. I mean, people have all got to die some time. It's sad, sometimes, you know, missing her. But I've got many fond memories and I know, because all her suffering is gone now, she is obviously more alive and radiant than she has ever been before. Her life was fantastic and that's what I like to concentrate on.

RR  So what do you think you have actually learnt from her death?

MB  I think I've learnt that there are times in our lives when we can't pray because we feel too sad, and some people say, 'Oh you know, is God really gonna help you if you can't pray?' God, in those times, he carries us, he doesn't always expect us to be top, as it were. He loves us and carries us and he knows people's sorrows.

The most difficult pain that many experience is the pain of bereavement. However many times you hear it talked about and however much you feel you may understand it, when it happens to you personally the pain is new and unique. To hear someone talking about the death of someone they loved can be both therapeutic for them and for those who take the trouble to listen carefully to what is said. One of the most memorable interviews I did involved the death of a child. They told me how they coped:

RR  Jackie and Stuart Potter have a young family – Aidan who is six, and the twins, Giles and Elizabeth who are two, but another child is still part of this family, Guy, the eldest son. He died of cancer when he was just four and a half years old.

JP  We were literally nursing him and reading to him

and it was very tiring and exhausting in all sorts of ways. I remember that Stuart had got up and I was nursing Guy, and Stuart walked round the garden, and I remember Guy turned to me and said, 'Mummy, I think Daddy needs a cuddle. I think we had better catch him when he comes back in, don't you?' Really, if a little boy who is so ill can be so aware of somebody else's feelings, I think it shows such a lot.

RR    What about your friends and relations? Did you find that they were able to help you or did they find it very difficult?

SP    People do find it difficult to enter into your situation. To help without feeling that they are going to upset you or to make the situation worse for you.

RR    So what would you advise people to do who are trying to help friends who are in similar circumstances to yourself?

SP    To keep in touch. To knock on the door and say 'How are you today?'

JP    Phone up. It doesn't matter when it is or what you have to say, but to do it is better than not to do it at all. Guy loved to see people. He appreciated it just as much as us, didn't he?

SP    To know that you are being thought about or that you are in somebody else's prayers is a very important thing.

RR    What about your faith? Was this a fairly shattering blow for you?

SP    Yes, it's shattering; there is no other word to describe it. I think, if anything, it has strengthened our faith because it has shown us that you can't be an entity. You rely very much on other people. We have gained a lot of benefits from other people helping us, sharing their faith with us.

SP    I think you do appreciate as well that when people say 'You are in my thoughts' or 'We're praying for you' that you get an awful lot of strength from that, just knowing that people care.

*150*

At the beginning of the book I mentioned an interview with actor William Roache during which he talked about the death of his daughter, Edwina. To hear someone talking about something which is so very personal is always a moving experience. It also helps to be able to sit down and read what was said:

**RR** How old was the child?

**WR** Eighteen months.

**RR** How did you cope with that?

**WR** Well, it was quite extraordinary because there she was, eighteen months, a perfectly healthy little girl. She had a little bit of a cold, snuffles like they've all had – we really panic when they get them now. She went to bed that evening a bit hoarse and we called the doctor, the doctor came around. My wife and I went out for dinner, my in-laws sat in, we came back, my wife went upstairs – she was fine at about eleven o'clock. Forty minutes later she went in, she was dead. It was so horrendous – the shock – we suffered a grief that went on for about five days and I remember saying to Sarah, 'I don't think I can stand this much longer.' It was a physical pain inside, I couldn't face anybody, I felt guilty, I felt wrong – you can't help it.

**RR** What sort of support were you and Sarah getting?

**WR** Well, we got tremendous support. The press, who are pretty horrendous most of the time, actually came to the door and said, 'What can we do for you?' and I said, 'Just leave us alone,' and they did. They were smashing, all of them. We got an incredible sackload of letters, unbelievable support. We didn't eat, we just drank hot chocolate, that's all we could get down. And we cried, and in between crying tried to ring people up, and burst into tears – it was awful, I just didn't want to see anybody. Then on the fifth day, or fourth morning I think it was, just before the funeral, I woke up and I saw Edwina's face glowing. I wasn't asleep, I know I wasn't, and I saw it in a light, like a halo around, a glowing little face smiling, and at that moment the grief went – I'm not saying totally, there will always be a certain amount, but that awful grief went, and I went through the funeral, because I was dreading it – I didn't think I'd be able to get through the funeral . . . it's horrendous, children's funerals . . .

**RR**    It's harrowing, isn't it, the funeral of children.

**WR**    . . . and, unless you've been through it, you cannot quite understand the physical pain of grief. But I, we did grieve very heavily for four days and then that little vision. Sarah, at the same moment, felt a sort of lifting, and now we try and make it a positive thing of appreciating the time we had with her. We have her photographs around, instead of that awful reminder of a tragedy . . .

**RR**    Yes . . . Edwina's not pushed away.

**WR**    Oh no, and I believe in life after death anyway – she's there, and we enjoy the short time she was with us.

When it comes to talking about finding strength through suffering there are few better to talk to than Dame Cicely Saunders of St Christopher's Hospice, in Sydenham, South London. The hospice movement has created a fuller understanding of Christian death. The dying person needs to be cared for, to be allowed to die with dignity, and to be as free from pain as is humanly possible. Certainly hospices try to do this. They also realise that someone who is dying is not an isolated individual but a person with friends and family who also need care. People who have possibly seen little relevance in the Christian faith have their eyes opened when they witness the devotion and dedication of a hospice.

Dame Cicely, in an interview on Palm Sunday, saw clearly the strength of the hospice movement and what it had to offer:

RR   So what are you trying to do, day in, day out, here at St Christopher's?

CS   Trying to see the very maximum that a person can make of this time, in their own choice and in their own way. Both in physical possibility – and there may be much more than you think, in the relationships with the people they love – and there may be much to do there, there may be reconciliations or there may be new understandings of each other; and also what they can do in looking at the meaning of their lives and what has been most important for them. So that they can be ready, when the time comes, in its own time, to lay that life down with a degree of peace and some satisfaction. I think what we want them to be able to feel at the end of life is that they can say, 'I'm me and it's all right.'

RR   This is total care though, isn't it?

CS   By a total team. It's not one person's work, it's the work of a group, the nurses, the doctors, the social workers, the chaplain, the physios, the orderlies, everybody else in the house, the back-up secretaries. We're a group focusing on the needs of an individual family and it's also, of course, the whole family, not just the patients separately.

RR   Now is it important that you're a Christian family doing this?

CS   For us it is. We wouldn't be here if we hadn't believed that God wanted us to do it, and that if we used every opportunity he would both bring the money and the people that were going to make it possible. But other people have come into this work with a different commitment – I think the commitment is basically to people and what is important about them.

Not everyone has, or gains, the strength of faith to cope with some of the suffering that they experience. Either religious faith has little meaning to them or the suffering that they experience actually shatters what faith they may have had. They find it hard to believe in a God that 'allows' such suffering to exist. They forget, or do not understand, the meaning of personal freedom and that a lot of the world's suffering is caused by the thoughtlessness of humans, rather than the arbitrary power of God. One place I visited, which showed some men's inhumanity to women and children, was a refuge in Middlesbrough. For obvious reasons the visit had to be kept quiet, as had the location where the interview was to take place. There what I heard was a stark reminder of the difficulties that some people have to face and all because of the suffering that one human being can inflict on another human being.

Suffering which is borne alone is often the most painful. If there is someone with whom you can share the burden of pain it is eased considerably. In many cases it is a strong faithful marriage that helps ease this burden. This was particularly true with a couple I visited in Hexham. The programme was to be the first in an Advent series of *Songs of Praise* and if ever there was an example of light overcoming darkness it was in the way Granville Campbell coped with disability:

RR      Granville Campbell was almost completely para-
        lysed in a car accident over twenty-five years ago.
        He still manages to lead a full life.

GC      At the time of my accident the most difficult thing
        was the sense of helplessness, only having limited
        use of my arms and not being able to use my
        fingers. Local charitable groups bought me a word
        processor computer and I have had to learn
        seventy codes of sucks and blow. Six years ago we
        bought an old Local Authority Range Rover
        ambulance. Margaret couldn't drive but she learnt
        to drive on the ambulance and so she's able to take
        me out. We don't need to go far outside Hexham to
        find somewhere quiet, and park, and be renewed in
        the peaceful surroundings.

RR      Have you changed as a person since the accident?

GC      Well, I'm not the person now that I was then and I
        have presumably grown spiritually and now reap

the benefits of the fruits of the Spirit – love, joy, peace, patience, even-temper, none of which I was before the accident. Other people seem to be able to want to tell us their troubles and our patience and somehow increased human understanding helps us to be patient and listen.

Grace Sheppard, the wife of the Right Reverend David Sheppard, expressed her feelings about suffering in her book *An Aspect of Fear*:

**RR**  Why was it so important to you to write *An Aspect of Fear*?

**GS**  Well, I'll take you back to the very first letter I had from the publisher, which was inviting me to write a book, and it was the way they put it that made me think I had something to say. I had no thoughts about writing about agoraphobia, about fear, about anything, and they used this rather long word, spirituality, and I thought, you know, what does that mean?

**RR**  It can be a blockage word.

**GS**  So I had to go away for a few minutes just to think about what that word meant and quite quickly I think I realised it had something to do with being alive, something to do with the human spirit, something to do with our feelings and how they connect with our concept of God, and so I sort of listed a few of those to myself and when I came across the word 'fear' I thought 'Ah, I think I know about that' and being a preacher's daughter and a preacher's granddaughter and a preacher's wife, I do realise it's important that when preachers get up to preach they don't talk above people's heads, but they – if they can – bring in some of their own experience to make it come alive.

**RR**  But this must have cost you quite a bit, because it was opening yourself up to people who didn't know you suffered in this way.

GS    Sure, sure. Yes, it did cost me a lot, Roger, but in a sense I had faced that cost before I got the invitation to write, the invitation came at the right time when I had already begun to face my fears and to get control of them. The cost now is that it's gone much more public and although that is costly – I'm proving that it was a cost which has brought a great deal of life to me and a great deal of life and freedom to other people.

RR    How important has your own personal faith been in coping with fear?

GS    Well, that is a good question, because I wasn't sure how my faith was going to come out through this book. And having written it I have a deep sense of gratitude that somehow my faith has come out to be very, very deep indeed and very real. A faith in God and Christ, the God who believes in being there for people. I think I had a rather lop-sided or incomplete sense of who God was before I started to write this. You know, on the one hand He was a God, a judge who was always ready to tick me off for not being perfect, and in a sense he was much bigger to me than the other bit of the God which I was worshipping which was Jesus, the friend; and I grew up with Jesus the friend, you know, to talk to him in prayer like a child talks to a very close childhood friend. But that judgmental God and that friend God had to come together for me.

Adrian Plass was another guest who was willing to talk about the mental suffering he had experienced. I was on holiday when he was on the programme, but he told Paul Jones of the ordeal he went through:

PJ    You really went haywire, didn't you? Why was that? What happened?

AP    Well, I think it was a combination of things, really, Paul. It was the work I was doing with children, although lots of other people work with difficult kids and don't crack up. I think I have to say mainly it was the Church. Not a particular Church, but – but my frustration with feeling that it had become a game and that I was taking part in a game that it was terribly hard work to join in with. I was becoming so spiritually arthritic that it hurt. I couldn't stretch mentally, or spiritually, and I think I just withdrew really from the effort of trying to make it real.

**PJ** So there is a darker and perhaps depressive side to Adrian Plass. Is that the thing that we so often seem to find in funny men?

**AP** I think it is certainly true to say that the diary – the *Sacred Diary* – for instance, came out of all the hurts and difficulties of that period. It poured out, literally. I mean I took a pen out one day to write the first bit – it was a column in a magazine – and out it came, like a flood. Yes, most really funny people I know, go home to darkness quite often.

**PJ** You say that the Church was part of it, and that your work with disturbed children or teenagers was also part of it. Where was God in all this?

**AP** Well, that's what I'd like to know and I'm going to have a very stern word with Him! No, I think that each of us is surrounded, if I may be metaphorical for a moment, by . . .

**PJ** Please be metaphorical!

**AP** . . . by a thicket, if you like, which is made up of temperament and background, and our own stubbornnesses and difficulties. I think God hacks away at that constantly and occasionally a passage is forced through and we are able to make some sort of contact. But I think we often feel safer within that little clearing we have got inside the thicket, and I think being born again, which is something we talk about very freely in the Church, takes years for some of us. The rocks need to be broken up and lots of work needs to be done. When I finally came through this time I remember it was Michael

Harper who said to me, 'Nothing has been wasted' and that was a wonderful thing to hear – sort of spiritual manure. All these dreadful things and mistakes and problems, all being ploughed back in to enable growth . . . new things.

Adrian's new-found health and strength have enabled him to become one of Britain's most popular Christian writers, and performances of his *Sacred Diaries of Adrian Plass* play to packed houses. His recent book *A Smile on the Face of God* tells the story of a priest, Philip Ilott, restricted to a wheelchair by multiple sclerosis. It closes with a remarkable development: a real life unexpected ending which took place after the book had been written.

Recent years have produced no greater campaigner for children than *That's Life* presenter Esther Rantzen. Child abuse was seldom, if ever, talked about. Then suddenly it became front page news. It is a subject which raises fierce emotions and yet needs handling with the utmost sensitivity. Esther realised there was a need to be met, so set up Childline, but her desire to care for the vulnerable had very deep roots indeed:

**RR**     But you have obviously got from your Jewish faith the family strength. What else do you feel that you have got from it?

**ER**     It could be that I am aware of the under-dogs, the losers, the victims. You see, when I was little – I was five when the war ended – people in my family, people in almost every family I knew had relatives who had suffered in concentration camps. If they had survived they were often mentally very damaged, and of course physically, and many of them hadn't survived. So I learnt very early on about the cruelty of humanity and the fact that some people suffer unjustly, and it may be that that has alerted me to people still suffering. And I cannot bear the unaccountable, uncontrolled use of power on the vulnerable, and for me I suppose abused children are an equivalent to what goes on in concentration camps, because the abusive adult has that child totally in his or her power, just as the concentration camp guards had their victims totally in their power. And I think that kind of racial memory – I hope doesn't make you paranoid – but just makes you terribly aware that there can be locked away suffering that the world prefers not to notice.

Damage that occurs at such an early age always leaves a scar which takes a long time to heal, and rarely disappears completely. The problem of suffering, especially what is called 'undeserved suffering', has baffled mankind for centuries. At times people have considered suffering as something to be striven for while others sought to avoid it at all costs. To me both views are unrealistic and I believe un-Christian. Suffering is a fact of life. It is not a punishment from God. And yet is has to be faced. What we see in both the life and ministry of Jesus Christ is that suffering can be changed into glory. The supreme example of that is, of course, the Cross and the Resurrection. It is also the theme that runs through the healing miracles and is the way in which many people were drawn to become followers of the new way in the Early Church.

Seeing the way in which people have coped with their suffering has always been a great inspiration to me.

# THE FOOD OF LOVE

If I said it once, I said it a hundred times – we don't do requests on *Good Morning Sunday* – but the message had very little effect. People still wrote for requests, and some even got quite cross when we didn't play the record that they'd asked for even though we had done their dedication. But what was obvious was that people listened very carefully to the music we played. Some of it they liked, some they didn't and if they didn't they were not afraid to express their feelings.

I had nothing whatsoever to do with the choice of music. The first time I heard many of the records was between 6.0 and 7.15 a.m. The stops and starts were played through to me or, as it's referred to in the business, we did the topping and tailing. On occasions I didn't like what was played but I was encouraged not to say so, so sometimes my reaction was couched in such terms as, 'Well that was quite a bouncy record for this hour of the morning,' or 'I've never heard that one before,' said in such a way that I hoped I wouldn't hear it again. I was given one piece of advice regarding my reaction to the records by John Forrest. He thought instant reaction to records wasn't wise and he was right. Often when I heard something played over while we were rehearsing I would give an instant judgment and yet, when I heard that same record in the context of the programme, my reaction was entirely different. I also realised that by criticising the choice of certain records out of hand it meant that I was criticising, not always constructively, the work of one of the producers. If that producer happened to be the same one that was on duty in the studio that morning it was not an ideal way to start the day.

The range of music was considerable. Certain artistes were always acceptable and fitted well into the Radio 2 ethos. It was very important to make sure that the programme fitted in well with the rest of the network's output. There is no point in putting out a programme which is simply a religious ghetto. Hopefully, people will tune in to hear Foster and Allan, Vera Lynn or Harry Secombe and then decide to stay to listen not only to the interview, but also the specifically religious music.

The vast majority of the music we played was Christian, but now and again we would play music that would mean a lot to people of the Jewish faith and, of course, we frequently played recordings of the Psalms from which both Jews and Christians draw spiritual strength. But in the main the music reflected the Christian faith. As a point of policy we never played secular songs that had as their theme either highly erotic, or sadly unrequited, love. All the secular music had to speak about positive love and happy relationships. The odd record did slip through the net now and again, but on the whole the producers were very faithful to that policy. When it came to choosing the religious music then the field was very wide indeed.

Hymns were part of the staple diet. There was always one before the 8.0 a.m. news which often reflected the time in the Church's year. Generally there were other hymns scattered about the programme. Many people asked to have their dedications linked to a hymn and quite a few would have liked to have had a programme that was wall-to-wall hymns. I was certainly glad that we didn't. Had we just had hymns we would only have attracted those people who were in tune with hymns; generally people who had a Christian faith already. By making sure that there was other music as well it meant that the programme was accessible to the enquirer, the doubter and even the non-believer and, who knows, hearts can be changed. Christians must be very careful not to turn their beliefs into the registration form for a very cosy club.

Clubs are fine for those who are on the inside but they can be very forbidding to those who don't know the secret code for getting in. Some Christians far prefer to tend to their own needs and see to their own comforts rather than fulfil the command of Jesus to preach the Gospel in all the world. Or if they do wish to fulfil this command, they want to do it in a very up-front and obvious way. With some people this approach will work but for many it is too much for them to cope with. They far prefer to be fed gently with milk rather than having to go straight on to the solids. I, personally, see nothing wrong with this providing that when people are ready for solids we are prepared to feed them.

Certain hymns were in-built troublemakers. Not because of the words but because of the tunes. 'Oh Jesus I Have Promised', 'Love Divine', 'The Lord's My Shepherd', and even my own favourite 'Just As I Am' were all fraught with danger because they all have more than one tune. So, although you pleased some people, there were always quite a few who were indignant that you hadn't played their tune, or as they preferred to call it, 'the correct tune'. For my last programme, when I was allowed to choose the music myself, Michael Wakelin took the trouble to get me to sing the tune of the hymn I had chosen over the telephone so that we ended on a happy and harmonious note. But even Michael Checkland, the Director General of the BBC who was a guest on the programme, didn't get the tune that he knew and loved for the hymn of his choice, and if the DG can't have his way, there is very little hope for ordinary mortals.

Guests were often asked to choose a hymn as one of the pieces of music we played during their interview. This proved to be a very useful way of getting the person to talk about their faith, especially if their faith was not deeply thought out or the major influence in their life. If an interviewee had little to say about their faith one producer seemed to increase the number of hymns in the programme. Presumably he did this on the basis that what was not conveyed in the spoken word could be conveyed in song.

There was another problem regarding hymns. Believe it or not, it is quite hard to find good recordings of many hymns.

Christmas carols are plentiful in all shapes and sizes. Cathedrals, mass choirs, parish churches and pop stars all try their hand at putting together the ever-popular Christmas album. But it is not easy to find such a variety at other times of the year. The Huddersfield Choral Society's excellent record of hymns saved many a situation, as did the choir of Seaford College Chapel, and a record which, in my running order, was just credited as 'Massed Choirs in Manchester Cathedral'. We had our own way around this problem. First of all, we were very fortunate to be able to book the BBC Concert Orchestra, under its leader Martin Loveday, to record a number of hymns for us. For these recordings they were under the baton of Noel Tredinnick, the Director of Music at All Souls, Langham Place. He is a former choirboy of Southwark Cathedral and a person who, through his *Prom Praise* performances, showed a great love for giving hymns the big orchestral treatment. Over the years he has created many stimulating arrangements of hymns and it was good to be able to share these with a wider public. There was one snag: the contractual arrangements that were made with the orchestra only permitted the recordings to be played twice. And, as you can imagine, recording with concert orchestras is not cheap.

As well as hymns being given the orchestral treatment they were also thought to be ideal subjects for the up-tempo beat of jazz. Chicago Classics did two sessions for us, taking well-known and well-loved hymns and playing them in jazz style. We received a number of letters asking whether these were available as commercial recordings but there were a few letters from people who really objected to the style thinking it not far from blasphemy.

The other source of good hymn singing was the Choirgirl of the Year. One of their competition pieces had to be a hymn and the winner was asked to include some hymns in the music that she recorded for the programme. Once again, we were restricted in the number of times we could play the recordings but when they were played they never ceased to please. The Choirgirl would also record secular music and this, once again, was a good way of blurring the unnecessary divide between what is secular and what is religious.

*163*

The most controversial music that we played was some of the modern Christian music. It was important to include this type of music in the programme otherwise those people who draw tremendous spiritual strength from it would have felt excluded. It is also good for people, whether they are believers or not, to learn that the way in which people express their faith is for ever changing. Some people didn't take easily to this music, but quite a few were more than pleased to find that after they'd heard it several times they began to like it. And for some it really was a relevant way to praise the Lord. With any music, be it contemporary or ancient, there are going to be some who love it and some who hate it; some who think it's good and some who think it's bad. But it is important that it is heard otherwise people start to believe that if it's not old, it can't be good. From the past we can learn a tremendous amount. To get rid of all that is old would be sacrilege, but it would be equally wrong to ignore what is new. Many people write off anything new as being trendy, especially if it is linked with religion. I find this a very offensive way of rubbishing the things of today. If you visit any of our great cathedrals you will find that every age has added its little bit to the building and this has, to my mind, increased the glory and the splendour of the original building. Yet, when it comes to music, anything of today is thought to be totally abhorrent by many people and, what is more, they think it shouldn't be heard. We tried to avoid music that was trite or unworthy of the programme but the producers worked hard to use that which was thought to be of a high standard. One of the contemporary singers who was extremely popular, especially with production assistant Tanya Astley, was the American Christian singer Don Francisco and I certainly learned to appreciate the music of John Michael Talbot.

One singer who can always get away with recording modern Christian music and still hold on to a traditional-loving public is Cliff Richard. Somehow he is able to bridge the gap and take people with him. Even those people who are repulsed by the very thought of a guitar, happily accept that guitar in the hands of Cliff. In his own concerts he shows that he approves of the *Good Morning Sunday* philosophy of music choice. In his secular concerts he often includes one of his Christian songs and in his Gospel concerts he uses all the modern means of production to stage a very lively show.

Music has always been important in the ministry of the Church and it was good to be able to include some meditative music. This was particularly appropriate when it came after the prayer slot. It also pleased Canon John Oates if that piece of music was from a record made by the choir of his Church, St Bride's, Fleet Street.

On outside broadcasts, if there was any chance of recording some local music, we always did. The pupils and staff of the Lord Mayor Treloar College did their bit for us, as did the Scouts when we were in Bath for St George's Day. Musicians in Lapland, Austria and Belgium contributed local colour to the programme. Again, the problem of broadcast standard reared its ugly head. The music that we recorded on location couldn't be done in a studio and so it was bound to be of a different quality from the commercial recordings that we played. But engineers did their best to produce the most balanced sound. As far as I was concerned local contributions were always well worth getting, but then I was not involved in the hassle of the actual recording.

Young voices always seemed to gladden people's hearts. In the early days, when the programme came every alternate week from Manchester, we played special recordings that had been made for us by the Great Moor Junior School in Stockport. The sound these children made was always refreshing and I was pleased that on one visit to Manchester I got the chance to call in at the school and thank them personally. When the programme had a Bristol base we did recording sessions with the Bristol Junior Choir, and they too made you feel better, just to listen to them.

Music can capture all the emotions. Many a letter I received said how listeners had heard a piece of music with tears running down their cheeks, while others found that another piece of music put a spring into their step. A lot of trouble was taken by the producers to choose the right music and it was time and trouble well spent.

# THE CHOIRGIRLS OF THE YEAR

Over many centuries the tradition has been, and still continues to be in most cathedrals, that choirs are for the male voice. The pictures on Christmas cards, the shots that appear on television, are generally of young boys in their choir robes looking angelic, their mouths wide open singing the praises of the Lord. In reality, things are quite different. They may have glorious voices but, despite the angelic look, choirboys are not known for angelic behaviour. Various games are devised to pass away the time during what they think are boring sermons; alternative reading material is tucked into the choir stalls and the cassock covers a multitude of sins. Also, in these days, choirboys are often in short supply.

There is, of course, no guarantee that girls will behave any better, but many Churches of all denominations would not be able to have a choir if it were not for the willingness of girls to volunteer. The producer, John Forrest, felt that this act of service should be recognised. For a number of years the boys have been recognised through the Choirboy of the Year competition organised by BET, the services company, whose offices are situated alongside the Royal School of Church Music, but girls had been completely ignored. So ever-inventive John set about rectifying the situation by inaugurating the Choirgirl of the Year competition.

It was thought necessary to find a sponsor and who more natural than BET. Through co-operation with them it was possible to provide the winner with a trophy and five hundred pounds, and a thousand pounds for the choir from which she came. The girls who came second and third received £150 and £75. The competition was open to all girls who sang in choirs or music groups and who were between the ages of twelve and seventeen. The problem then was publicity. Notifying Churches is not always the best way of drawing something like this to public attention. Somehow this sort of information is coupled with trash mail and finds itself in the vicarage black-plastic-dustbin bag before anyone has even glanced at it. Obviously it was possible to publicise it on *Good Morning Sunday* and this, of course, we did to good effect. Additionally, it was thought sensible to link up with local radio stations so as to get as much national coverage throughout the British Isles as possible. The local radio stations and the national radio centres in places like Cardiff, Belfast and Glasgow responded, some with more enthusiasm than others, and the girls were encouraged to send in their tapes.

Barry Rose, the then music adviser to the Head of Religious Broadcasting, headed the selection panel listening to numerous tapes and selecting the eight finalists. Once I had recorded the promotional tape for the competition I had nothing to do with it until I met the finalists. The task of selecting them took many hours and had to be done by professionals so that a high standard was maintained and all competitors were to feel that they had been fairly treated. Barry Rose was the ideal chairman of the judges. Not only is he a musician of high standing, but he also has great experience of church music and choirs in particular. Through his work at Guildford Cathedral, St Paul's Cathedral, King's School Canterbury, and St Alban's Abbey, he knows better than most what is expected of a chorister and what to look for when judging such a competition:

RR     Was it difficult choosing the eight finalists?

BR     It got very difficult in the end because we listened to over sixty cassettes which were the final submissions from the local and regional radios, and then we had to work out from that eight finalists.

RR     What were you actually looking for?

BR    Somebody who communicates through their sing-ing, not necessarily somebody who's got it totally all right and just leaves you a bit cold, but someone who actually communicates the meaning of what they're singing because this is the job of the singer.

RR    Now you have specialised, I know, particularly in the past, with boys' voices. Do you find the girl's voice as good as a boy's voice?

BR    Now there's a difficult question, you've put me into a minefield straight away. In fact, I do work at the moment with boys and girls mixed up in the same choir – yes, they are as good, but there is an age difference, I think. I would stick my neck out and say that a well-trained boy of thirteen sounds about the same as a well-trained girl of about sixteen.

RR    So you have to be very careful as you get that mix?

BR    Yes, I mean, in the school where I work, we are at that stage where we have boys who are finishing their treble career at about thirteen, and girls of sixteen and seventeen, and each complements the other's strength.

RR    But you find some choirmasters who just will not mix them at all. Do you think they're being rather stubborn on this?

BR    No, I don't think so. I think if you're able to get boys, you know, in your locality, that's a very good thing because I think there are many things that ladies and girls can do, but one thing they will never be are tenors and basses, and you have got to look to the future, of not only singing in churches, but in your local choral society, or the sort of people you find singing in any choir.

Barry Rose, of course, was not the only judge. Mrs Rosalind Runcie, a keen gardener, a music teacher and the wife of the then Archbishop of Canterbury, was also per-suaded to join the judging panel. She obviously enjoyed the experience because the next year, when she was not able to be a judge, she joined us for the finals despite attending the funeral of her mother earlier in the day. She said that she knew she would find the atmosphere helpful to her in her bereavement and from her comments afterwards she certainly did.

Mrs Runcie is also familiar with what is expected of choirs. In her capacity as a musician she is well aware of the demands that are made upon them and as a worshipper at many special ecclesiastical occasions she realises how much beautiful voices contribute to the glory of the worship. She also realised the value of music in a person's life:

**RR**   Rosalind, you have been teaching the piano for a number of years, haven't you?

**R**   Yes, as long as I can remember.

**RR**   Do you encourage young people to learn the piano?

**R**   Well, it depends on the child. Somebody comes to me and says, 'Can I come and learn with you, my friend is learning with you?' – I never advertise actually, it's just word of mouth – and I say, 'Well, it's boring learning the piano, there's such a lot of learning to do, are you prepared to work hard? Because if you're not then I don't want you,' and that actually sometimes firms them up, so to speak. They think, 'I'll show her.'

**RR**   It's a good way to challenge them. But do you feel that you were taught well as a child to appreciate music?

**R**   It was always there, we had a piano and my father was the son of an opera singer. I wasn't even asked if I wanted to learn the piano, I was just sent for piano lessons, and that's the best thing that ever happened to me.

**RR**   What about young people today? Do you think on the whole they are encouraged to play the piano or do you think they are told to just play the record player?

**R**   Well, I don't know. I think first of all when television came out I thought, 'That's the end of anybody wanting to do anything' but frankly you, on the radio and on television, have done so much to show people what live music is all about – I mean look at the competitions you have and look at this one today, it encourages people, I think, to try for themselves, to learn something. This is the most wonderful thing because when everything else fails – I have a niece who said to me, 'Art doesn't let you down' – people do betray you, they say nasty things but music is always there, it's the same, it's waiting for you. I feel passionate about it.

To be a good singer, especially in a competition, you need to be a good performer. A beautiful voice is essential but so is the way in which you project that voice and project yourself. Two of the judges that we used knew this only too well. Marti Webb and Aled Jones both know the demands that are put on a performer, whether they are singing solo or as part of a choir. They too told me what they were looking for:

RR      Aled, what do you look for in a choirgirl as regards her voice?

AJ      Right, well I've never done this before, so I'm a bit nervous. I think I'm more nervous than the singers. I'm looking for performance, more than anything I think, and in the performance of course of tonal quality, diction, but more than anything a comfortable performance.

RR      Now you were an ordinary choirboy, and then became a performer and a choirboy.

AJ      Yes.

RR      How did that change come about?

AJ      Well, it's a very difficult change because when you're singing in a choir, you know, you don't stand out, but as a treble you've got to have something different. As a singer you've got to have something that stands out so people instantly recognise your voice. But with me that just came about naturally. But I'm looking forward to hearing the singers today. I've heard they're very, very good, so . . .

**RR**    They're super, they're super. You obviously had to choose music for your records and things like this, what advice – I mean it's too late now, but what advice would you have given them about choosing the pieces of music that they will be singing.

**AJ**    Well, not to choose a too difficult piece of music because in a competition as well, when one is always nervous, it's always difficult to perform a difficult piece. But then again I see someone singing Fauré's 'Pie Jesu' which is, maybe not a complicated piece but a very difficult piece to sing, because you can go sharp or flat – it's also a very slow piece so it's very difficult to perform.

**RR**    I always used to go flat.

**AJ**    Same here.

**RR**    One of the other things – I know because I've met both your parents on different occasions – they've been a tremendous support to you.

**AJ**    Oh very much so, yes.

**RR**    What would you say to parents of these girls?

**AJ**    As you said, my parents were a great support. They didn't push me at all in what I did, you know I chose my own music, I – my own concerts – so I suppose for the parents of the choirgirls to emulate really, is not to push them into anything they didn't want to do. Because it's very difficult to sing in a concert you don't really want to sing in, or if you're feeling ill with a sore throat or if you've got a cold, and it's always better not to sing than to struggle out on stage because people are always too ready to criticise a bad performance.

Marti Webb began by telling me about her experience with competitions:

**RR**    Did you ever go in for singing competitions?

**MW**    I did when I was about ten, but I was useless and

they gave up. I think it was at my little local school, the singing teacher really thought that I had something. She was lovely, Miss Best, and she would try and enter me for these singing competitions and I used to get, 'Lovely voice, no personality and must smile' because I was always petrified. I was useless.

**RR**    When did you get over that hurdle and realise you could perform and sing?

**MW**    I don't know, I think it was when I went to stage school and they really more or less ignored you and let you take your own pace and your own time. Eventually I felt a bit better. I'm still petrified now whenever I sing, but you learn to cope with it better, I think, that's all.

**RR**    But do you find it difficult to combine both the acting and the singing, because I mean you've done so much acting with the singing?

**MW**    I think the acting helps the singing. I never think of singing, I only think of acting, so I concentrate and somehow the singing does its own thing – it comes along with it. Which I think helps with the nerves because then you concentrate more.

**RR**    What do you think makes a good singer, Marti?

**MW**    I don't know. A good singer, I don't think, necessarily means to have a fabulous voice. A good voice is something that's very pleasant to listen to in any way, shape or form.

**RR**    What advice would you give to some young girls who haven't got a Miss Best or a Mrs Best as their teacher to encourage them, to get them singing properly? What's the best advice you would give them?

**MW**    I think to enjoy it. If you enjoy it, I'm sure it will work somehow, but I mean, I've never had lessons as such, so I'm not a trained singer. It all depends on the sort of voice you have or the sort of voice you want. If you want to be a trained singer, like if you want to go into opera, or even into choral singing, I think you must have lessons to train your voice.

The Royal School of Church Music has played a very important part in both setting and maintaining the standards of church choirs. Through their training schemes and their courses they have been able to encourage what are quite ordinary choirs and choristers to offer their best, and often the end result has been quite thrilling. Success, of course, isn't always guaranteed but at least if choirs are encouraged then there is the chance of something exciting happening, as I heard from Janette Cooper of the Royal School of Church Music, who was one of the Choirgirl of the Year judges:

**RR**    What is the Royal School of Church Music?

**JC**    It's an institution to further the performance of music in the context of church worship.

**RR**    Now what sort of stress do you think is put on a chorister these days? I have to admit, Janette that I never made Head Chorister, so I don't know the stress involved. What stresses does a chorister face?

**JC**    Largely, I believe, that of commitment, because if you take on a job as chorister you are committing yourself to regular attendance, and that means regular work. If you are being led in the right way, then it will be enjoyable work, but regular it must be.

**RR**    What qualities will you be particularly looking for in the finalists?

**JC**    I would like the singers to be able to persuade me immediately that I can put aside pencil and paper, forget that we are talking in terms of competition here today, and just to sing, to make music to me.

**RR**    That seems a slightly selfish thing – what about the rest of the people?

**JC**    Very selfish, but everyone else is going to get their own picture. Now the same person may not be a turn-on to other people around me, but I want this to be a personal something between me and them.

*173*

**RR**     Do you think, then, there's a great danger in competitions that really it does become the three judges and their likes rather than the likes for everybody?

**JC**     Of course, because music is not a science, is it? Music is an art, there is bound to be an element of the subjective in this. But I hope that all of us here are going to enjoy everything of what we hear today and, human nature being what it is, there will be one winner. We have really got eight winners here.

The setting for the competition was the beautiful Wren church of St Bride's in Fleet Street. This made ideal surroundings, not only because the church itself was just right for the competition but because we were able to use the crypt and vestries for interview rooms, judges' rooms, changing rooms and, most important of all, a base for the engineers with all their equipment.

In its first years the competition went out live to most local radio stations and as each competitor was introduced the announcement always included the radio station from which she came. Sadly, in later years, the local radio stations ceased to do this though the whole competition was still recorded because parts of it would be used the following morning on *Good Morning Sunday*.

Neither John nor I are great lovers of competitions. They can set person against person and a highly unpleasant atmosphere can be created. Fortunately, with the Choirgirl of the Year competition, this didn't happen. The girls seemed to enjoy what they were doing and, supported by their families, friends and often their choirmaster or mistress, they were willing to share in the success of the occasion, even if it didn't mean personal success for them. In some ways the age range of the competition made it difficult for some of the younger entrants as they naturally did not have the experience of the older girls. But I remember one girl, Joanne Burton, who was very young when she entered the competition and yet did exceedingly well. So well, in fact, that she was a finalist two years running. Many of the girls came armed with mascots, some of which showed signs of being much-loved, and although on occasions there were tears they were really tears of exhaustion and excitement rather than tears of disappointment.

Each girl had to offer two pieces of music, one of which had to be a hymn. The intelligence and clarity with which they sang would put many a congregation to shame. Dressed in a variety of choir robes they would hold both their books and their heads high as they tried to convey the meaning of what they were singing. As regards the second piece of music, the range of choice was very great. Some chose to sing a piece which they had obviously sung in either the school or church choir, whereas others chose a special piece which they thought would show their voice off to its very best advantage. Some pieces were well known, while others were something new and some, on occasions, original.

When the girls arrived at St Bride's on the Saturday morning they were given time to rehearse. In Peter Wright, who was then at Guildford Cathedral, and Andrew Lumsden of Westminster Abbey, they had very sympathetic accompanists. As they put the girls through their paces they gave them every bit of encouragement. While these rehearsals were going on I would be sitting in the crypt of St Bride's doing interviews. I asked each girl why she had entered the competition, what it meant to her, and what she had chosen to sing and why. Obviously it was my aim to put the girls very much at their ease. It was enough having to sing in a competition without going through the ordeal of a radio interview. In the main they coped extremely well and it was a delight to listen to their responses.

After lunch at the BBC canteen in Bush House, the home of the World Service, we all returned to St Bride's for the competition itself. A little time was given for the competitors to digest their food. Many of them were very impressed with the high standard of BBC canteen food after having heard over the years so many broadcasters complain about it on air. Once the competition started it ran through without a hitch. Those competitors who were at the end had the benefit of having the standard set by the other girls, but they also had the strain of waiting for their turn to come. As each girl returned to her seat, having made her musical offering, you could see the great look of relief that came over her face. Now and again there was the odd grimace as they remembered back to a wrong note or some bad breathing.

Once everyone had sung the judges withdrew to their room and the rest of us headed for tea, organised in a local hostelry and hosted by BET. Although the food was always good and the amount generous, it was never an easy meal to digest. There was that slight feeling in the air of 'if only'. Typically, all that the girls could remember were the mistakes they had made. They seemed to forget the overall delight they had brought to those of us who had listened and had admired their performances. Fortunately adoring grandparents and parents were all on hand only too ready to accentuate the positive.

By the time we returned to St Bride's the judges had made their decision. Barry Rose, as chairman of the judging panel, would always give the overall assessment of the competition, normally including a statement of how, yet again, the standard had been higher than the previous year. In typical competition fashion the names of the winners were announced in reverse order; the Choirgirl of the Year being announced last by the Controller of BBC Radio 2 and presented with her trophy and cheque by the Chairman of BET, who also happened, coincidentally, to be a church-warden at St Bride's. Before she could really relax and enjoy her award she had to sing again. And so the competition ended with the joyful sound of a young lady who was about to face quite a busy year.

We were very fortunate in our winners, for not only did they have lovely voices they were also delightful people. The very first winner was Victoria MacLaughlin from Northern Ireland. She, her parents and her music teacher were thrilled with her success. For me there was an extra benefit which I didn't expect. With Victoria coming from Northern Ireland I mentioned to her how much I enjoyed soda bread. From then on a regular ration used to appear, which did nothing for my weight but certainly delighted my tastebuds.

As well as the trophy and the cheque, the Choirgirl of the Year received a contract to record eight pieces of music to be used on *Good Morning Sunday*. I had nothing to do with the arrangements for these recordings but I always appreciated the end results, and so did the listeners. The delightful sound of a clear young voice early on a Sunday morning was a glorious way to start the Lord's day. But the winner's voice was not just heard on *Good Morning Sunday*. Radio 4's *Daily Service*, *Blue Peter* and *Songs of Praise* on BBC1 also booked the choirgirl to appear. Actually, I was sorry that *Songs of Praise* didn't make more use of the choirgirls as I'm sure the viewers would have both enjoyed seeing and hearing them.

And, of course, in their own local area they were very much in demand, especially for charity concerts. Victoria has gone on to study music to take it up professionally, but for the second winner, Sarah Cox, music and singing were much more of a hobby. Sarah came from Lancaster but her father was unable to be at the competition because he was working in Canada. Obviously, after the competition was over, Sarah telephoned her parents to tell them the good news. What Sarah didn't know was that we had arranged for her father to speak to her live on *Good Morning Sunday* the following day. At the end of the programme, when we played the recording of the previous evening's announcement of the winner, I did a short interview with the Choirgirl of the Year. As I was chatting to Sarah I told her that I had someone on the telephone who wanted to speak to her – it was, of course, her father. The look of sheer delight that came across her face was glorious to see and just added to the happiness of an already very contented young woman.

In 1988 the Choirgirl of the Year was Sarah Ryan. Sarah radiated happiness in both her face and her voice. The piece of music that she chose to sing was 'Count Your Blessings' and it really couldn't have been more appropriate. I spent a very pleasant evening at Sarah's school when the cheque for the choir was presented. The school made a wonderful occasion of it; they staged a very enjoyable concert which, of course, featured Sarah. It was also good to hear the hymn which Sarah sang for the competition being sung again. Although it was well known, 'All Creatures of our God and King', the tune was new. It had been composed by Michael Davey, the music master at the school and an excellent tune it is.

I met up with Sarah again when I went to Newark parish church for a Christmas concert. Over the years this concert has been organised by one of the local doctors, Victor Twyman, and a wonderful occasion it is too. He is brilliant at getting local schools, choirs and soloists to contribute. He's also good at persuading a few outsiders to become part of the Newark family, if only for one evening. He had persuaded me to compere it and unbeknown to me he had also invited Sarah. As usual she sang beautifully but she also had to suffer because during the singing of the 'Twelve Days of Christmas', she and I had to sing a duet. Like Victoria, Sarah also hoped to make music her career. This can never be an easy decision to make because, as well as the joys of making music, you have to face the knocks of a highly competitive world. But if your heart is set on it then you have no alternative.

The last Choirgirl of the Year that I worked with was Ruth Fortey from the United Reform Church in Sutton Coldfield. Like Sarah Cox, music for Ruth is a hobby, but both she and her Church were delighted that she had reached such heights. The choir that she belonged to is called Jas, and its name was proudly carried on her T-shirt. As well as making some beautiful recordings for *Good Morning Sunday* I was soon getting letters from people asking me to publicise the fact that they had managed to persuade Ruth to sing for them and so, hopefully, raised more money for the charity they were supporting.

Competitions come and go but I hope the Choirgirl of the Year competition will remain for a long while to come. It does take an enormous amount of organisation. The finals are only the icing on the cake; a great deal of work has to go on before those events happen. But as a competition it is a way of displaying the very high standard of music that young women offer to the Church and it gave listeners of *Good Morning Sunday* the chance to hear, especially recorded for them, some beautiful fresh voices which otherwise might have been enjoyed only in their own local area. The one important thing is that the atmosphere of the competition continues to remain pleasant. Setting people at one another's throat will not do good for God, man, woman, or music.

# THAT COMPETITIVE URGE

There are some people who thrive on competition. I am not sure that I do. It could be something to do with the younger brother syndrome – but we won't go into that now. The world of entertainment is a highly competitive world and with competition goes insecurity. One minute you are loved by everyone, the next no one wants to know you. The old saying that you are only as good as your last show is very true. It may well be that you have a contract which lasts a year, as I did for *Good Morning Sunday*, but when that year is coming to an end you still wonder what the future holds. I felt very unhappy with the way *Songs of Praise* arranged their work. I would get a letter at the beginning of a series stating which programmes they wanted me to present but that was no guarantee that I would be presenting them.

Living with the insecurity was a good lesson in faith. For years I had been preaching it, now was the time to practise it, and I realised that preaching and practice could be two very different things. Certainly it kept me on my toes, as did the continual assessment of my performance. Listening and viewing figures are all-important for every kind of broadcasting – religious programmes included. Each month, with *Good Morning Sunday*, I would hear how things were going. Fortunately, in the main, they got better and better but the programme is also assessed for its Reaction Indices. The RI is an appreciation figure based on questionnaires completed by people on a listening panel who are randomly selected. This, at times, could be a very detailed analysis of the performance of the programme. People's reaction to the choice of music and the quality of guest is recorded as is their reaction to the presenter. This was the first time I had ever had my work looked at in such a way and although at times it could be painful it was also extremely useful. I realised that certain mannerisms irritated some members of the audience greatly, and although I never wish to be bland it was also important not to be unnecessarily irritating. However, scholars were and are still very divided as to the enjoyment level of my laugh.

What, of course, irritated one listener might be enjoyed by another. I always signed off *Good Morning Sunday* with 'See you next week, Cheers.' Now, I had several letters from people complaining about the use of the word 'Cheers'. They said it sounded as though I was in the spit-and-sawdust bar of the Pig and Whistle and was about to show my gratitude to someone who had bought me, yet another, round of drinks. This they thought was totally unsuitable for an early Sunday morning religious programme. But the expression 'Cheers' is very much part of me so I continued to use it. In the end I was glad I did because a year or so ago I went to a local *Songs of Praise* for the younger families section of the Mothers' Union in Ashford, Kent. Just as I was leaving I was collared by one of the ladies who said that whenever her late husband went out he always said 'Cheers' to her, and so to hear me say it each Sunday morning brought back to her very many happy memories.

Competition makes you sensitive to the demands of the market. Sometimes it is right to give in to those demands, sometimes you have to try and point to something better. Although competition is very human I am not certain that it can be thought to be divine. Competition can lead, very easily, to jealousy and envy and once those emotions, or to give them their more accurate description – sins, take over then you have a very fragmented society. Jesus had to tackle this with his own disciples. The moment that James and John (or was it their mother?), asked for chief seats in the Kingdom of Heaven the fat was in the fire. 'Why should they have preference over us?' thought the other disciples and Jesus was faced with getting everything back into perspective. If we only competed against the standards set by Jesus then competition would be very good, our weaknesses set against his perfection. But we don't behave like that, we prefer to compete against other humans, setting our weak standards against their weaknesses. It is no wonder that it often ends in tears.

Hopefully, the competitions we ran on *Good Morning Sunday* didn't end in tears, although obviously they did, at times, end in disappointment. That was certainly true with the biggest competition we ran. Nearly five thousand people entered the competition to win an Easter cruise in the Mediterranean with the *Good Morning Sunday* team and Swan Hellenic. It was a prize well worth winning. It was run in conjunction with the *Radio Times* and competitors had to answer the following questions:

1. In which town did Jesus heal Peter's mother-in-law?
   (*Answer: Capernaum*)
2. The Apostle Paul's travelling companion on his first Missionary Journey was Barnabas. Where was Barnabas born?
   (*Answer: Cyprus*)
3. In the Bible the Sea of Galilee is called by three other names. Give two of these.
   (*Answer: Sea of Chinnereth, Sea of Tiberias, Sea of Gennesaret*)
4. Bishop Jim is a regular guest on *Good Morning Sunday* and he will be joining the cruise as a lecturer. He is Bishop of where?
   (*Answer: Stepney*)

There was a little bit of confusion over Barnabas but on the whole most people who entered got everything right. The names of the winners were drawn out on air but I was determined not to do this alone. Had it just been for a bar of chocolate or an autographed photograph then possibly I wouldn't have worried, but a holiday of a lifetime is something different. Fortunately, Rabbi Hugo Gryn was willing to stay on after he had done the prayer slot so he drew one winner and I drew the other. The next week on the programme I spoke to both the winners, live on air. One of them hadn't slept a wink for fear of what I might ask and what they might say. But the winners turned out to be highly appropriate as Ron Wootton, from Northampton, had always wanted to take his wife to Athens where he had been in the war and Paul Mitchell, from Walton on Naze, was a lay preacher and felt his ministry would benefit from a visit to the Holy Land. They also made very good broadcasters, when, on one of the programmes we did from the cruise, we involved them so that we could hear their reaction to what they were experiencing.

One of the brightest competitions we ran was devised by production assistant Tanya Astley. She had the great idea that we should run a Listener of the Year competition. It was a sure way of finding out whether people were actually listening to the programme or were just using *Good Morning Sunday* as background entertainment. It was also a useful test to see whether people were actually hearing what was said or heard what they wanted to hear. To answer even three out of the ten of Tanya's first draft of questions you would have needed a doctorate in the study of *Good Morning Sunday*, but by the time the quiz went out to the listening public it had been modified somewhat. But even then some of the most avid listeners failed the test.

So that we were able to select an outright winner we used the ploy that many competitions use – state in not more than twenty-five words why you listen to *Good Morning Sunday*. Brian Forman of Burton on Trent, who was the winner, came up with this sentence: 'I listen to *Good Morning Sunday* because it unites people of all denominations and circumstances in a little haven of warm and sincere fellowship. Music is an extra treat. Thank you team.' His prize was an all expenses paid trip to the *Good Morning Sunday* studio on 31 December 1989 where he was interviewed by me on the programme, presented with his trophy, and had a special photograph taken which he later received framed. There was also another surprise for him. Before we left to have breakfast together he was presented with the first ever pair of *Good Morning Sunday* bedsocks. Though this is not quite in the same league as a trip to the Mediterranean, Brian Forman and his wife certainly seemed to enjoy themselves.

The most instructive competition on the programme involved a Bible Garden. The listener could send for ten packets of seeds, all of which would be plants that were mentioned in the Bible. Obviously they had to be seeds of small plants which could be grown in a window box or a few plant pots; not all the listeners to *Good Morning Sunday* have ten acres of ground in which they can grow a biblical plantation. The *Good Morning Sunday* offices in Bristol and London tried to set a good example by growing the seeds themselves, but sadly the plants didn't always receive the tender loving care that they needed and the grass withered and the flowers faded. Alongside the actual growing of the plants came instructions, not necessarily on how to grow them but rather of where in the Bible the plants were mentioned. To instruct us in this horticultural Bible Study there is no one better than Nigel Hepper – Principal Scientific Officer at the Royal Botanical Gardens in Kew. I had never visited Kew Gardens, even though at one time the entrance fee was only 1d (in real money, before decimal currency). As a place it is fascinating to visit but my visit was made even more enjoyable since Nigel was my tour guide. Within the gardens he pointed out to me some of the biblical plants:

RR    What is so special about this sunken garden area, Nigel?

NH    This is a protected area where the sunshine can make the plants grow to good effect, and it's arranged with little neatly-cut box hedges, and then there's also the myrtle tree. There are two forms of the beautiful myrtle and if I pick a little bit you can smell it – it has a lovely fragrance . . .

RR    Oh that's lovely, that is gorgeous.

NH    Yes, you see, it has little glands and this lovely oil in it. Now the box tree and the myrtle are referred to, at least in the Authorised Version, by Isaiah as being the choice shrubs that will grow in the desert in the day of the Lord.

**RR** Now why particularly would these be so good in the desert?

**NH** Well, they're all evergreen, you see, and in the desert there are so many thorny and leafless plants. And here's this lovely, fragrant, beautiful green plant.

**RR** What about this, Nigel? What have we got here?

**NH** Well, there's the sage, several species of the sage. Now this reminds us of the lampstand of the Tabernacle, the Menorah. It is said that the form of the sage, its branching, gave the idea for the branching of this candlestick or lampstand.

**RR** So the special Jewish candlestick is based on the sage?

**NH** Yes.

**RR** I never knew that before.

**NH** And if you read about it, there's also mention of the flowers of the almond, and the almond trees are flowering now in many parts of the country. It's a lovely flower and of course that was well known to the Israelites too.

**RR** Is there anything else particularly biblical? You were mentioning something about mustard seed, and of course that comes from one of the parables of Jesus.

**NH** Yes. Yes, well that tree, the little one over there, is the Black Mulberry. Now this is referred to by the Lord as Sycamen and he told the disciples: 'If your faith is even as small as a grain of mustard seed then the Sycamen [or the Black Mulberry] would be rooted up and planted in the Sea and it would have ailed.'

**RR** Now did you find in your own faith as you were examining things in the garden that this grew and developed?

**NH** I found the accuracy of the Scriptures remarkable

in relation to the plants. I mean, some of the plants are difficult to identify, the flowers of the field and so on, exactly what they were, but there are so many that are dead accurate. I mean, we mentioned the myrtle, for example, did you know that Esther, Hadassah, the name of Esther is the myrtle?

**RR**   No, I didn't realise that – amazing, so you get the names as well. We are learning a lot this morning.

Each month he would come into the studio and we would learn a little more about the seeds we were sowing. Fortunately, with Nigel, this was not just an academic exercise. As a member of the Gideons not only did he have a great interest in the Bible, and had written a book on plants of the Bible, but was also a man of deep faith. Even those who were not able to grow the seeds learned a lot from his monthly talks.

Many photographs arrived in the office of those who had put heart and soul into their Bible Gardens. Sunday Schools had made it their project and it was obvious that the interest spread far further than the *Good Morning Sunday* audience. Interest in the project was increased when we announced the poetry competition which we ran in conjunction with the Bible Garden project. Listeners were asked to write a poem about the seeds that had been mentioned on the programme. This was not an easy assignment. Many people were fond of sending me poems, some of which they had written, some of which they'd enjoyed reading themselves and wanted to share the enjoyment with me. Writing a poem to order is far more demanding. The competition was judged by Nigel Hepper and the author Brian Sibley. On the programme in which we featured the winning poem Nigel stated why they had won and Brian, as well as commenting upon them, read them for the listeners to hear. The two winning poems were:

**My Bible Plants by Sidney Turner**

Rose of Sharon, O what a Name
Emblem of Jesus' Heavenly fame.

Bright as the sunshine's lovely display
Filling the darkness with the light of day.
Peace of the olive please give to me
The oil of all goodness and purity.
Seed of the mustard grow in my heart
Help me to flourish and do my part.
Fruit of the vine refreshing my soul
Cleanse me from evil till I am whole.
Sadly the palm and the apple tree die
While herbs of the field just multiply.
Seed of the anise, beautiful taste,
Pungent flavouring too good to waste.
Flowers abundant and of all hues
Christ the 'lily' is the one I choose.

## Flax by Jannette Stanworth

All the glorious blue of Heaven is reflected in her face,
And the beauty of the Godhead in her slender, fragile grace;
She is truly blessed of flowers, for she grew where Jesus trod
And her dainty, waving blossoms graced the pathways of her
    God.

Her stems became the lampwicks in the houses where He
    stayed,
Or the sails of Peter's fishing-boat, the nets that Andrew
    made,
The curtain of the Temple came from fibres that she grew,
And she felt the crucifixion as the curtain rent in two.
But how blessed she was by Heaven, oh how privileged, how
    proud
When her threads became the basis of the linen of His shroud.

So celebrate the crocus, or the cumin or the dill,
The hyssop or anemone, but yet remember still
That the flax is truly blessed of flowers and grew where Jesus
    trod
And her dainty, waving blossoms graced the pathways of her
    God.

Other competitions were far lighter in comparison and were really just for fun. On most of the seaside special programmes we would ask the listeners and those who were with us at the actual recording to make a sentence using as many letters as possible out of such things as 'Bournemouth Pier' or 'Blackpool Pier'. So as to start them off, each guest who appeared on the programme was asked to enter the competition and to submit their sentence. Here we did cheat. So as to make life a little easier for the celebrities they were given a sentence which had been thought up by the resourceful mind of whichever researcher was working on that programme.

As well as competitions that were linked to seaside specials, we generally made sure that on every outside broadcast there was the chance to win some little souvenir. Once again, it was a way of involving people, particularly the housebound listener, or the listener who felt they were too old to travel but still wanted to share in the excitement that travel often brings. Generally these competitions were based on information contained in the programme.

We were always very well aware that *Good Morning Sunday* must never become another 'record-and-dedication' programme. There was the need to make sure that it contained some real meat. Sometimes this was easier to do than at others. In Lapland we had to make sure that we were not just another holiday programme. When we visited Israel we had no such problem. At Passover time Jews have always said 'Next year in Jerusalem', and many Christians have looked to the Holy Land as the one place they have longed to visit. So many listened with extra interest when the programme came from there and the competition on our Easter Day programme from Jerusalem in 1989 had questions which demanded that people listened attentively.

Another competition I ran involved stories from 'the mouths of babes and sucklings'. Children have a habit of saying things in a very fresh and direct way. This is frequently true when they want to question the reality of God and their relationship with that which is eternal. Parents do their best to make things as simple as possible and even the most theologically astute mother can find herself in difficulties when it comes to telling a four-year-old about belief in the life everlasting. One story I received for the competition faced this very real problem.

An elderly relative had died and a young boy was anxious to know exactly what happened when a person died. He was told that the body was either buried or cremated, but the soul went to heaven. This satisfied him for a short while but then he wanted to know exactly what the soul was. His mother explained that the soul was part of the body which you couldn't see and it was that part which went to heaven. In another part of the kitchen his younger sister was playing but obviously listening attentively to this conversation so she added to the discussion, 'Mummy, I can't see my botty. Will that get to heaven?'

While we were running the competition, and it proved a very popular one indeed, I read out three stories each week and declared one to be the winner. The stories were nearly always of a high standard and certainly I enjoyed the one that came from Mrs Peggy Steadman of Sandhurst, Kent. Apparently Peggy was at a family service and at the end of the service there was, of course, the blessing. Peggy wrote: 'We came to the blessing and the rector said, "Let us pray." There was a big sigh behind me and a heartfelt four-year-old voice filled the church with "Oh, no, not this again."'

Mrs Fletcher from Harrogate had a wonderful story to tell about her grandson, Jonathan. On one occasion, when he was five years old, he was taken to see his Gran and apparently he misbehaved. To his great surprise, he got a really good telling off from Gran. He looked at her in amazement and said, 'If I was my mummy I wouldn't bring me to see you!' With that, poor Gran collapsed not knowing what to say.

The winning story that particular week came from Joanie Carpenter of Hampstead, London. She wrote: 'It was bedtime and as usual my mother was busily supervising the bedtime rituals. We said our prayers and mother was tucking in the blankets around my little brother and then myself, when my sister said thoughtfully, "Mummy, if Charlie tucks Teddy into bed, and you tuck in Charlie and Babs, and Daddy tucks in Mummy, and the guardian angels tuck in Daddy, and God tucks in the angels" and here she paused for a moment "Who tucks in God?".'

I suppose my favourite little story concerned a very crippling illness. When talking about something from which people suffer you have to be very sensitive but I think that no one could really be offended by this story. Sadly I no longer have a record of who sent it to me. It concerned a young girl who returned home from school in a very agitated state. She said she had to take some money to school the next day to give to the teacher and it was urgent. The teacher was going to plant sixty-five roses and unless she gave the money, someone would die. When next morning the mother took the little girl to school, although she didn't doubt her daughter's story, she thought it was a little garbled so took the opportunity to have a word with the teacher about the sixty-five roses. The teacher herself was baffled until she realised that the previous day she had told the children that they were going to take a collection in class for those who suffered from *cystic fibrosis*.

To my knowledge we never received any complaints about competitions on *Good Morning Sunday*. This may well have been because the competitions on the programme were mainly for fun, even if at times the winnings were well worth having. However, competition in life should often carry a government health warning since it can certainly damage your health both physically and spiritually when it is taken too seriously.

# YOURS SINCERELY

I greeted Thursday evenings with mixed emotions. At about six o'clock a despatch rider would arrive at my home with a bundle of envelopes. One of them contained the dedications for the next Sunday's programme, two would often include what we term 'general letters', and another two would contain invitations to speak anywhere around the country and letters in connection with offers that the programme might be running at that particular time.

When I started presenting *Good Morning Sunday* there were generally only about three letters each week. To string these out for over an hour and a half was not easy but I would resort to snippets from the newspapers, people's birthdays and special historic anniversaries. It was at this time that my friends found themselves frequently being given a name-check, although at times their names were changed to hide their identity. Somehow the idea that people could have a record dedicated to them caught on. By the time I finished presenting *Good Morning Sunday* there was never a Sunday when I was able to mention on air all the letters I'd received.

Obviously, although it was not possible for me to do requests, I tried to make sure that the letter was linked with a suitable record. I once heard a story about a disc jockey on Radio 2 who was given the sad news that Bing Crosby had died. Knowing how much the listeners appreciated him he thought it was only right that he should play one of Bing's records. Having made a suitable tribute to the work of the great entertainer he cued in the record – 'Cheek to Cheek'. What he had forgotten was that it opens with the words, 'Heaven, I'm in heaven'. It could have been worse.

In the early days when all the letters could be included I took a lot of time matching record to dedication. Once I had more letters than there was time for on the programme I realised that there had to be a change of policy. The production assistant who opened the letters in the office put them in date of arrival order so that it was possible to adopt what I felt was the only fair policy of first come, first served. Obviously some letters were given special treatment. Anyone who was a hundred years or over was brought to the top of the pile. If they got a letter from the Queen they should certainly get greetings from *Good Morning Sunday*. Diamond weddings tended to be given the same treatment. I also cast an eye to see if young children had written. I had mixed motives in doing this. It encouraged younger people to write and at the same time increased the number of people listening to the programme. Trying to broaden the age range of the listeners was always of paramount importance as it was vital to appeal to as wide a range of people as possible.

Once I sat down with the list of records to be played on the programme, I would start placing the dedications after the eight o'clock news. When that section was full, I filled the seven thirty to eight slot. There was only one time that I really regarded as mine and that was before the record, always a hymn, which took us up to the eight o'clock news. Frequently people would write asking for this time for their dedication but it was a time that I jealously guarded. It was the time when I felt I could be more reflective. It was the time when I would pray about any recent tragedy, like the *Marchioness* disaster on the Thames, which occurred earlier one Sunday morning; or the Hillsborough football disaster from the previous afternoon. Often it was a time when I could include a dedication which had a strong note of sadness. It was so much easier and I think more helpful to the listeners for this sort of event to be linked to a hymn rather than to a piece of music which could have been considered unsuitable. It was also the time that I used for my private dedications. When my Nanny was seriously ill and dying in a hospice, it was at this time that I told her that I was thinking of her. It was also one of the ways in which I could thank the staff who were caring for her. Possibly this was usurping my position as a presenter, but I was never told off by my producers and from the comments I received from listeners they seemed to value sharing part of my life with me.

One other piece of queue jumping was for people working on the programme, especially those working on it that particular morning. If one of the team had a birthday or if one of them had a close relative celebrating an anniversary that day, I thought it important to include their dedication. This was particularly true for members of the team who didn't even get a regular thank you at the end of the programme.

I never minded opening the big envelopes that contained the dedications because I knew all those letters would be friendly. A letter I shall always be grateful for was one from a man who said that he thought that at seven-thirty each Sunday morning the whole of Britain became one parish. This was an atmosphere I tried to create and I was thrilled when I felt that it was recognised by someone else.

At one time I thought that the vast majority of dedications were for people celebrating their Ruby wedding, forty years of happily married life. These dedications became so popular that I thought I was sitting on top of the EEC Ruby Wedding Mountain. I got real withdrawal symptoms, which were quite difficult to handle, when I found I had a programme without a Ruby wedding dedication. Then, of course, dedications for the other wedding anniversaries flooded in. Anniversaries like, Silver, Ruby, Gold and Diamond, I knew – the complications set in when the letters mentioned times like Paper, Crystal and Emerald. Here I was in difficulties but, as always, one mention of the problem on a programme and it wasn't long before some helpful listener had written in with the anniversaries listed, alongside the number of years they represented.

As well as the dedications for the longer-lasting marriages, there were also letters from proud parents wanting to rejoice in the anniversaries of their offspring. The only complication for these letters came when it was the bride's mother who was writing to me, because more often than not she would forget to include the married surname of the couple and so I had to hope that the people in question would recognise themselves. There were also dedications for those with second marriages. It was particularly lovely receiving a letter from someone asking for a dedication for their third wedding anniversary, when they went on to say that they were seventy-nine and their partner was seventy-six and that they had both been very happily married before but both their previous partners had died. However, they had both now found happiness in their new love. This gave me a thrill because it is a sign that not everyone experiences continued loneliness after the loss of a partner. These letters generally contained thanks to both families for all the support that they had received and that delights the heart.

It soon came home to me that while many rejoiced over the length of their marriage, a great number did not. Obviously, those who experience divorce have a particular loneliness, as do those whose partners have died. I didn't receive a great number of letters from those who had been divorced, but from widows and widowers they poured in and I hope I encouraged them. Hearing dedications for those who were still married where both partners were still alive was not that easy for them. So I suggested that they wrote in for a dedication saying that had their partner still been alive it would have been their Ruby or Golden wedding anniversary. From the letters I received and people I met in the street I realised that this was a great help. By a mention on a radio programme we helped to turn what might have been a sad, empty day into one which was somehow special. Being mentioned on the radio has knock-on effects. Friends you haven't heard from for years get in touch and an atmosphere of celebration takes over. There is that feeling that the person has become a celebrity. Most importantly the person has been recognised.

Fundamentally this is the Christian faith. If, as Christians, we do believe in life after death and hope to share Christ's resurrection then there is nothing wrong with remembering those who have died. The Salvation Army, of course, refer to death as 'gone to glory', but I do believe that some of that glory can be reflected here on earth when we remember in love those who have died.

Often it was good to be able to include dedications which reflected church life in Britain. Sometimes there is an impression of the Church, as an institution, dying on its feet, while those who belong to it become more and more disillusioned and gradually drift away. From the letters I have received the opposite is the case. Of course, there would be a lot of letters from people telling me about particular church functions, wanting a little bit of free advertising in the hope that they would raise a little more money for their roof, bells, organ, tower etc. Knowing how difficult it is to raise this sort of money, I was only too pleased to be able to help whenever I could. However, the letters that I really appreciated were those which reflected both the growing life of the Church and the dedication of those who were members of it. *Good Morning Sunday* was interdenominational and represented the whole span of Christian life. Adults being baptised, young children being confirmed, those making their first Communion, babies being baptised or dedicated: all this showed that time and again people were being added to the flock. Although there is still room for many more, the continuing growth is healthy.

Long-standing faithful servants of the Church were never forgotten. I hope I realise, as much as any clergyman, how vital the volunteer is. Worship would be very dull without music and in most Churches music needs organists and choirs. It was good to receive letters from Churches wanting to thank their organist or a particular member of their choir for the wonderful service that they had given, often over many years. One piece of significant news that I had to give out was the retirement of an organist whom I knew very well. Leslie Kercher had been organist of St Peter's on the St Helier Estate, in South London, for at least twenty years. He was organist there when I was a curate. He had a great feel for worship and couldn't have been more adaptable to the needs of choir and congregation. I received a letter from a member of the choir telling me that there was to be a special evening service to mark Leslie's retirement and they wanted all former members of the choir to get in touch. There was a lovely response, not just from the broadcast but from members of the congregation chasing up old friends, and even possibly a few lost souls, and a marvellous service to the glory of God and in thanksgiving for Leslie's musical ministry was held. Being St Peter's the service was naturally followed by a party in the hall. St Peter's is not a parish to miss a knees-up.

Bell-ringers, vergers, sacristans, churchwardens, sidesmen and -women, elders, deacons were all remembered from time to time thanks to the letters I received. It is so easy for these people to be forgotten. They often work behind the scenes and because they are efficient and cause very little fuss they are more often than not taken for granted. It has also been good to remember those who help care for the young within the church community: Brownies, Guides, Rangers, Cubs, Scouts, Venture Scouts, along with Boys' and Girls' Brigades, and other young people's organisations which have featured quite prominently. Often people remembered with thanksgiving their Sunday School teachers. I remember one letter which asked me to send birthday greetings to an elderly lady. This lady was now in a nursing home run by two people whom she had taught in Sunday School. It was lovely to see the cycle of care going full circle. Also, by mentioning all these people, I hoped that as well as thanking them for their very often sacrificial service it would encourage others to volunteer. The effect of that I shall never know.

Only rarely did we do 'Where are you now?' dedications. These letters had to be handled with care. Unable to give out full addresses on the radio, we had to make arrangements for people to write into the BBC first. These letters often contained quite confused messages and it was difficult to sort out the relevant details. Without having a 'Where are you now?' spot as such, it was obvious from the letters I received that frequently we renewed friendships which had lain dormant for a number of years.

At one time a sad postcard used to arrive quite regularly. It was from a father sending birthday and Christmas greetings to his two children. Reading between the lines, this father was separated from his children because of divorce and was either denied access or because of distance found access impossible. Again, a dedication of this kind had to be treated with care; I had no idea how the children would react on hearing such a dedication.

With the number of letters received each week it was impossible to include all of them. At the end of the programme I would hand back to the production assistants the 'not dones' or the 'turn downs' as they were referred to, and those people would receive a letter saying how sorry we were that we were unable to include their dedication and trusting that it hadn't spoilt their day. It also suggested that they wrote earlier next time so as to stand a better chance of being included. This made a lot of work for the PAs but it was worthwhile, since people realised that their letter had not just been thrown into a wastepaper basket.

There was one other problem with dedications. Thankfully, some people were totally dedicated Radio 2 listeners. I have even seen Radio 2 put down as a hobby by one particular listener, or at least getting dedications played on Radio 2 as a hobby. This meant that those people knew about getting the dedications in early. They also knew how to write a dedication so that they caught the eye and were easy to read. One listener went to tremendous trouble and his dedications were always extremely well presented. Some also had at the top of the card a sticker saying 'Radio 2 is the best'. Although they are as entitled to dedications as anyone else, it is important to make sure that newcomers to the programme don't get overlooked. As many of those dedicated fans or avid listeners to Radio 2 were at Ray Moore's thanksgiving service, it was good to meet the people behind the regular dedications and explain to them the situation.

It was always possible from the letters to build up a picture of the listener. Many were elderly with hands crippled with arthritis but all seemed to be people who wanted to look to the positive side of life. It was good to share this optimism with them. I also learned where people were between seven thirty and nine on a Sunday morning. Many of course were still in bed, often enjoying their first cup of tea. Some were up having breakfast and one lady who wrote regularly did the ironing while listening to the programme. A great number of people were getting ready for Church. I would often be asked to do a dedication before a certain time because at that particular time they had to be out of the house if they were to arrive at their place of worship before the first hymn. As I sat in the studio it was good to get that picture of Britain on a Sunday morning.

The letters which arrived in the 'general' envelope had to be cared for in an entirely different way. These letters were not asking for dedications although quite a few each week would be saying thank you for dedications that had been done, and telling me how their celebrations had gone. If the dedication had been associated with a wedding quite frequently I would also receive a piece of cake in one of those little boxes. It was good to receive those letters.

A lot of people who wrote became very regular correspondents. They obviously enjoyed writing and as they felt they knew me through the programme it was only fair that I should know something about them. But by the time I finished the programme I felt I knew everything about them: their families, their friends, their Churches, and of course, if they had any, their pets. Obviously, it would be wrong to mention any individual names, but I have to say that there were a couple of Ednas who kept me very well informed. One of them, although housebound, seemed to have a very wide circle of friends; some of them even introduced themselves to me as being 'a friend of Edna' and this they thought gave them a respectability which they would otherwise not have had. I knew of the times when they weren't feeling that well, or were having problems that needed a little sorting out and which they wished to share with me. Obviously, there was little I could do practically but it does always help to share the sorrows as well as the joys. Other regular writers would, once a month or so, drop a line and let me know what they were up to.

Some letters would comment on particular programmes. It could well have been something I'd said or a contribution by one of the guests to the programme. People listen carefully to their radios and are interested in all that is being said. Quite naturally they want to join in the conversation and the only way to do that is by dropping me a line. Most of the letters agreed with what had been said and were frequently generous with their compliments. However, this was not the case with every letter.

It takes a while to get used to a new voice on radio and so in the early days I received quite a few letters from people who didn't enjoy the way I did things. Some of the comments were polite and helpful, some were abusive. Some people find change of any sort difficult to cope with, especially when they feel they have made a friend of the previous presenter. However, I was quite surprised at the way some people could put pen to paper in such an abusive manner. I would have thought that having vented their spleen on that sort of letter the best thing would have been to tear it up, rather than spend good money by putting it in the post. Some of these letters were anonymous and without an address. I know this kind of letter is cowardly and despicable and although these letters were always torn up and thrown away, they still hurt.

I felt that the letters which were signed and had an address, even if they were abusive, demanded a reply. Often, though, their criticism contained some truth. Sometimes it was the way they expressed it that was difficult to cope with. Often, if there was a telephone number on the notepaper, I would phone the person, usually from my own home. If this caught the writer on the hop I thought it was good for them to know that it was a person who had actually received their letter and one with feelings, and not a machine. One Saturday I telephoned two men who had written to me. When I spoke to them I seemed to have difficulty in getting my point across to them. I ended the calls on the basis that we would have to agree to differ. Interestingly enough, from both these men later in the week, I received letters explaining their attitude. One had just been made redundant and the other was far from well. I then realised that I had been a safety valve; they had had to let off steam to someone and I seemed to be as good a person as any. I was pleased that they took the trouble to write.

Some criticism was very humorous. There was one gentle-man who took the trouble to count the number of times I said 'very'. It is a word that comes easily to me. His letters were most amusing as he, of course, had included as many 'verys' as he possibly could. People seemed to give up trying to correct my pronunciation of various places when they realised the moment I saw an 'r' or an 'l' I was in difficulties. They also seemed to be accepting of the various stumbles. On the whole I tried to speak at speed, and this means that if I started to stumble over a word then the whole sentence clashed together with a pile-up of words that resembles a contra-flow on a foggy day on the M1. Some people were very helpful because they would give me pronunciation guides when it came to their name or the place where they lived. I have to admit that this didn't always guarantee success.

I did have one let out when it came to pronunciation and that was through people's handwriting. Far be it from me to criticise anybody's handwriting, mine is appalling, but at times I did wonder whether some of my correspondents were writing English. Some looked as though they had taken a course in early Chinese and were wanting to practise their skills by writing to me. Requests to print essential details, like names, went unheeded by the vast majority.

Some people have taken an instant dislike to me and nothing I've said or done has changed their attitude. These people didn't always write to me. They wrote to my bosses. Fortunately, I was well supported, but it has made me sad to think that some people have such hatred in their souls. When someone has decided that they can't stand you, you can do nothing right. It surprised me that they chose not to use the fundamental switch on any radio, or television – the on-off switch. With the growth of channels they might have decided to re-tune somewhere else. But they didn't. They preferred to suffer and object.

Some letters would criticise the Christian faith or the Christian Church, never difficult to do. Some Christians would criticise my interpretation of that faith. I was very sorry to receive letters objecting to the fact that *Songs of Praise* came one Easter Day from the Roman Catholic Cathedral in Westminster. One writer believed Britain to be a Protestant country and thought that on the most important day in the

Christian calendar the programme should reflect Protestant belief. This is a narrowness which, I believe, does the preaching of the Gospel no good at all, especially as that particular programme couldn't have been a better witness to the risen Christ.

There is one word that I don't use on *Good Morning Sunday* and that is the word 'luck', and this was because of a particular letter I received. I had either wished someone good luck or I had just said that someone was lucky – can't remember which. This writer pulled me up and explained that the word 'luck' should not be part of the Christian vocabulary as it denied God's power. I took the point. Another phrase I steered clear of was 'have a fit'. On a *Pause for Thought* I mentioned that my mother, who originally came from Manchester, would have 'had a fit' if she thought that I was flying to and from that great northern city. She would have thought that I had got above my station in life, that trains had been good enough for her and they certainly should have been good enough for me. One listener thought that this was a very careless use of words and she wondered if my mother suffered from epilepsy, and if not, then it was very inappropriate that I should describe her as 'having a fit'. From that letter I soon realised that I had to take care over the way I used my words. But some people had very raw sensitivities and would sometimes take offence where none was intended. Fortunately, I was seldom reprimanded by the sexist-language lobby. On the whole I seemed to get that right.

A lot of letters I received in the 'general' bag were letters asking for help. It could be that their choir had just made a cassette and they would like my comments, or better still for it to be played on the show – that gift was not in my power. I also received a fair number of poems, some of which showed considerable literary skill, and many of which obviously came straight from the heart, but I had to dash any hopes of being able to get them published.

The letters I received from people who were worried about their faith often revealed a considerable amount of misunderstanding and confusion. Some lived in total fear of God, expecting and experiencing what they saw as his punishment.

With this it was important for me to reassure them that although none of us can forget or ignore God's judgment, the Christian God is also a God of life who wants His people to grow rather than to be crushed. On many occasions I had to suggest that these people went and talked things over with their local priest or Christian minister, as it was impossible to deal in depth with all the topics raised in the letter. It would need a whole correspondence course and even that wouldn't be as good as being able to talk something through face to face.

Some people, in their often very long letters, told me of their personal problems. When I read of the difficulties people faced I realised how fortunate and protected many of the rest of us are. Some may well have got into difficulties through their own fault but this, if anything, made the pain greater and the need for help stronger. Once again, it was not possible to deal with such problems by letter. So, on some occasions, I would write back and get that person's permission to put them in touch with a local person who could help. Once I received this permission I then had to find someone locally who was suitable – through various networks and grapevines. I have to say how grateful I am to those people for their willingness and the thoroughness with which they did care. This really has been an example of practical Christianity.

The sad side of many of the letters I received was the tremendous feeling of loneliness that they revealed. People whose parents had died, or left them, people who had never had a partner, people who felt far removed from their families, often feeling that they had no one to turn to. Some felt they couldn't share their worries with the people they knew in case they were shocked, offended or embarrassed. So, instead, they turned to someone who they could look on as a religious 'agony uncle'.

Often just putting pen to paper helped them and they were certainly cheered by a reply. In many cases such people rarely receive any personal correspondence, all they receive are bills in brown envelopes. To receive a white BBC envelope, personally addressed, helps them to feel that they are of value, that somebody cares.

None of this correspondence would have been possible if my pleas for help had gone unheeded. As the letters began to pour in I found it more and more difficult to cope with them on my own, and yet at the same time I knew it would be wrong to ignore them. As I got further and further behind with my responses, I became increasingly worried until I was given someone to help me. Daphne Filshill had been a secretary at the BBC for some considerable time and had recently retired. However, she was willing to do some part-time work and very kindly agreed to help me. Each week I would dictate on to tape my comments on the contents of the letters I'd received and Daph would then turn them into a letter, well written, beautifully typed and properly punctuated and paragraphed. Without Daphne the service to the listeners would have been impossible to maintain. To me it was an essential part of the programme.

# LOLLIPOPS

Lollipops in life are essential; there must always be something to look forward to. Something which is just that little bit out of the ordinary that adds some colour, even some glamour, to what at any other time might be thought to be an ordinary, routine life. So many people who live alone and some who have disabilities of one sort or another find that their lives lack lollipops. Very often it is as much as they can do to get through the day and what are looked on as lollipops by others, like Christmas and birthdays, are often days to be dreaded by them. It was important on *Good Morning Sunday* to make sure that we produced some lollipops that were within the grasp of everyone.

BBC lollipops have to come within certain restrictions. They mustn't be seen to be an extravagant use of the licence-payers' money and so must fit comfortably within the programme's budget. They must also be in keeping with the ethos of the programme. Although some people might like it, others would find the thought of our giving away miniature bottles of gin highly offensive.

Of all the lollipops, the one I found the most fun was the one which most resembled a lollipop – the Roger Royle stick of rock. Once again John Forrest had put his fertile mind to use and had come up with this idea. Forgetting the damage they may do to teeth, he ordered a batch of rock made in yellow and green, the then Radio 2 colours, with the name 'Roger Royle' going right the way through. They were made at that Mecca of seaside rock – Blackpool – and when we did the seaside special from there we, naturally, paid the factory a visit. I never knew that rock-making was so fascinating. It is also utterly hygienic and it certainly seemed to be loved by those who received it. It was given away at our seaside specials though I must say that 'freebies' seem to bring out the worst in the British. Although I would generally distribute the sticks by throwing them to the four corners as well as the centre of the audience, there were those people who would knock down anyone who got in their way, and those who would ask for more, even if they'd managed to catch several already. As always, there were the meek who showed no signs of getting any rock let alone inheriting the earth. They waited patiently, hoping that someone might be generous and give them a stick. And, of course, there were also those who wouldn't touch it with a bargepole. They had been warned about such things as a child and that warning had stayed with them for the rest of their lives.

Scarborough saw a lollipop that brought delight to the audience. The weather couldn't have been better; it was the ideal day for ice cream and the local firm called Jaconelli's had made us some. Naturally, it too was in Radio 2 colours.

The moment that I mentioned to the Scarborough audience that we had some free ice cream, a queue formed. The British never seem to mind queuing, but what they do mind is getting to the front of the queue to be told that it has run out. At this stage any thought of peace, love or understanding goes for a burton. Mr Jaconelli had been extremely generous with the amount of ice cream he had made but it wasn't unlimited. There could be no re-run of the miracle of the Marriage at Cana on the sea-front at Scarborough.

Other lollipops were nowhere near as delicious but they were extremely worth while. The first was the Radio 2 teacosy. This was made in the shape of an old-fashioned radio and although not many people had kitchens in either yellow or green there were a lot of people who longed to become proud owners of such a treasure. To get one you had to recommend a teapot that you felt really deserved it. I received hundreds of letters, most of which have now been destroyed, but I did keep some of the letters and postcards.

Joan Veale from Totnes nominated another Totnes resident for a teacosy. She wrote 'My nominee for a teacosy is ninety-five-year-old Miss Emily Angel of Totnes. She lives up to her surname, has a multitude of friends who call to see her and who never leave before having a cup of tea. She lives on her own, is a registered blind person and is very deaf. She never complains, she loves to chat and has a strong Devonshire accent. Emily would be tickled pink to receive a teacosy.'

Mrs Maureen Papworth from Grantham wrote to suggest Mr and Mrs Stan Foster who had turned out to be marvellous neighbours in her hour of need. Mrs Papworth writes, 'They are always so kind and helpful and make everyone welcome. I don't know if you remember, but I have MS and recently my husband had to go into hospital. Stan didn't hesitate to cover the evening visit because they realised that it was too much for me to visit twice each day. Joy was very willing to stay with me although I was determined to cope. They lead a very busy life with a shop, WI, St John's Church and Scouts. With Joy and Stan it is just no trouble. They help people whenever possible.'

According to Mrs Sheila Gerkin, there was a little lady in Battle, called Mrs Miller, who also deserved to be considered. 'Mrs Miller suffers very badly from arthritis but is always so cheerful and kind to whoever enters her little flat and has given me many a delicious cup of coffee and cheered me up after my Friday morning shopping in town. Her beautiful pink geraniums in her window give lots of people pleasure too.'

Mrs Barbara Baker of Rochester nominated Mrs Dorothy Wallman for one of the teacosies because she said 'In spite of having a disabled husband and a handicapped son she is always there for tea and sympathy and helps a lot of people.'

Sometimes people nominated others for teacosies as a way of making up for past misdemeanours. Mrs Gail of Romford nominated Mr A. Warner because, she said, 'I invited a friend who loves the sound of the organ to come and hear me play. Unfortunately, I got carried away and three hours passed before I thought of offering the poor man a cup of tea, so one of your teacosies would make amends for my thoughtlessness. He is a great tea lover and we enjoy your programme very much.'

The card that came from Mr Topping of Corwen in Clwyd, nominating Mrs Andrew of Mostyn in Clwyd, painted a very beautiful, idyllic picture. He wrote, 'I am very pleased to nominate Mrs Norma Andrew of Mostyn for your attractive teacosy. Norma has a teapot warm for all callers at her little land-side cottage. There is a welcome for anyone whether calling for fruit, eggs or vegetables, a friendly chat, a little help or just a talk by the fire. I think Norma well deserves the nice surprise of a new teapot cosy.'

There were, of course, people who nominated relatives for a teacosy. Mrs Dorothy Summerfield of Hornchurch in Essex nominated her sister's lovely china-flowered teapot because she said 'her husband bought it for her in the thirties from Woolworths for 6d. Yes it's cracked inside but there's not one chip outside. Lovely shape, very pretty roses and fern. I am sure with a lovely teacosy they would make a delightful pair.'

And Gordon MacKay of Romford in Essex nominated his daughter-in-law for a teacosy because he said that during his wife's long illness and subsequent death last year 'she was untiring in her concern, help and love and has been ever since, to myself, despite having two young babies also to look after.'

You didn't have to nominate someone else for a teacosy, you could nominate yourself for your own collection, and two people who did that were Mrs Pauline Larrad of Draycott in Derby and Meg Edwards of Cable Street in London. Mrs Larrad wrote, 'Can I nominate one of my collection of 120 plus teapots? Possibly the most battered French one from World War One which survived its giver, or the oldest which is pre-Victorian. My husband, partially disabled by a stroke and a former ambulance driver, helps me to pack and transport them to talk on their histories etc, to clubs, mainly old folk, in the area. I don't charge and I get an enormous response of interest and memories from my audiences. Can you imagine their interest in your teacosy?' And Meg Edwards wrote, 'I have a teapot that would like a new cosy especially one from *Good Morning Sunday*. This teapot was given to my mother when she was married in 1910. I am now seventy-five and I can still remember that teapot when I was a child. It is still used now so you can see this old teapot would be very proud of a new cosy.'

It was always very sad when it was impossible to respond to all those letters, but I hope that as people listened and heard about other people receiving teacosies they didn't feel jealous; that instead they felt grateful that at least someone's teapot was being properly covered.

On outside broadcasts people who contributed to the programme in one way or another were often given small mementoes – keyrings, car stickers, or simple flapover pens – and they were appreciated by those who received them. Even children, who may well have preferred something which carried the Radio 1 logo, seemed quite contented to get a Radio 2 balloon. Doubtless it didn't last long but at least it served its purpose. The people who actually appeared on the programme and who weren't getting a fee were often given a proper Radio 2 pen or even a Radio 2 watch.

One lollipop was strictly restricted to five hundred listeners. When it was decided to launch the *Good Morning Sunday* cruise on the *Orpheus* in conjunction with Swan Hellenic, we realised that there would be many listeners who couldn't even contemplate the idea of joining us. For some it would be too expensive and many others would feel sick at the thought of a fortnight at sea. So there was a great danger of this trip being seen to be exclusive. John Forrest came up with the idea of the Cruise Companions. This meant that those who were unable to come on the cruise, for whatever reason, would still be able to feel part of it even sitting in their own armchair at home.

First they had to register as a Cruise Companion. It was a matter of first come, first served. Having registered they received a pack which consisted of such things as a deckplan and a postcard of the *Orpheus*, a detailed itinerary and notes of three of the places that we would be visiting. During the transmission of the programmes I would suggest that the Cruise Companions consulted their notes or checked the deckplan when I mentioned where we were on the ship. While we were away, I would send a postcard to each Companion. On the last trip the postcard was a very beautiful one of Galilee. Fortunately, through modern printing methods, it was possible for me to write one card from which the rest could be copied, but they looked as though they were all individually written. From the letters I received some people obviously did think that I had written them all personally but I have to assure you that the main work was done, first, by Hilary and then Jenny, who had the job of sticking all the addresses onto the cards. It was lovely to know that the cards had brought such pleasure. Some thought the picture so lovely that they went to all the trouble of framing them.

On our return each Cruise Companion was sent a little present. A lot of time and effort went into finding something suitable. It had to be small, and it had to be relatively cheap. On the first cruise we found some cards which had on them pressed flowers from the Holy Land. On the second cruise we found something which proved to be very popular indeed. These were small, mother of pearl crosses made in Bethlehem. We bought them at the Scottish Hospice in Jerusalem and from the many letters I received the gift meant a tremendous amount to their recipients. Sadly, despite a great deal of trouble being taken over packing, a few were broken in the post, but listeners with determination had got out the glue and done their best to repair the damage. At a recording of the fiftieth anniversary programme of *Sunday Half Hour* it was good to see a Cruise Companion who had already bought a chain for the cross and was wearing it with pride. With the cross went a letter that I had written telling the Companions that we had all arrived back safe and sound and saying that I hoped that they had felt part of the cruise, even though they had never left the comfort of their own home.

The last lollipop that I was associated with before I left the programme were the *Good Morning Sunday* bedsocks. Once again, they were in the glorious colours of Radio 2 and bore the *Good Morning Sunday* motif. Listeners had to nominate someone for them, someone whom they felt really deserved the comfort of these bright feetwarmers. On the whole the allocation of the bedsocks was fairly closely guarded. Whereas some of the teacosies had been sent for raffles in aid of charity, the bedsocks were sent only to individuals.

Anyone celebrating their hundredth birthday, or in one case their 104th birthday, automatically got a pair, as did people celebrating their diamond wedding anniversary. I thought that if they were getting a tele-message from the Queen they ought to be getting a pair of bedsocks from *Good Morning Sunday*. Actually, word got back to me from Westminster Abbey that the Queen herself had shown some interest in the *Good Morning Sunday* bedsocks. As regards the other recipients, each week I would select three letters from the vast number that I received, read them out on the programme, and the following week those who had been nominated would receive their bedsocks. On the programme we had a special slot for the bedsocks; it was generally at about eight-fifty and was introduced by some gentle snoring. Who was actually responsible for the snoring I never found out but it made an effective introduction to what became a very popular item on the programme. Once again, my only sadness was that it was impossible to give everyone who was nominated a pair of the bedsocks because the letters that I received were always very touching indeed.

Some, however, were fortunate. Lilly Carr from Plumstead nominated Mrs Bryan of Bermondsey for bedsocks when she wrote, 'I am wondering if you could send some bedsocks to a wonderful senior citizen of ninety-five? Mrs Bryan is a wonderful Christian lady who has made at least a thousand vests for babies in the third world and has also knitted other items for deprived children. She is a very modest lady and has thought of others for years. Her circulation is poor now and some Radio 2 bedsocks would make her tootsies warm.'

Mrs Lamb of Rickmansworth also wanted some bedsocks sent to a person as a way of showing appreciation for all that she did. 'I would like to nominate Mrs Francis of Rickmansworth for a pair of *Good Morning Sunday* bedsocks. She is a member of the WRVS and is the most caring person I have ever met. She is the organiser of the local Darby and Joan Club and arranges various activities weekly for the Club members. She also cooks for the Meals on Wheels service voluntarily and delivers the meals on specific days. Apart from these regular duties she shops for those people who are housebound, takes members of the Darby and Joan Club to doctor and hospital appointments where necessary, and takes in and collects prescriptions, sometimes without a word of thanks. Once a week Mrs Francis does voluntary work at the Michael Sobell House at Mount Vernon Hospital, which is for terminally ill patients. Her cheerfulness and willingness to help anyone has endeared her to all those with whom she comes into contact. My life has been enriched through being in contact with her.'

But often people who were nominated for *Good Morning Sunday* bedsocks were those experiencing a lot of suffering, and it was thought that a pair of the bedsocks would certainly cheer them up. From Mrs Brighouse in Orrell, near Wigan, came this letter, 'Could you please send a pair of bedsocks for my daughter's girl, Jenny, who has cerebral palsy and has never been able to walk or talk and also has a curved spine? She will be so grateful for the bedsocks for her nineteenth birthday.'

This letter I received from Totton, Southampton, for someone slightly older. Mrs Lillian Tanner wrote to me asking whether she could nominate Miss Winifred Plenty, also of Totton, for a pair of the *Good Morning Sunday* bedsocks. She wrote, 'Winifred is seventy-six, lives on her own and is badly handicapped with hip trouble and suffers a lot of pain. She cannot get out and manages the few steps indoors with a walking stick or pushes a tea trolley to get from room to room to help her along. She has no central heating and her legs and feet are often stone cold. She will be thrilled to receive your bedsocks as she always listens to your programme and watches you when you are on television.'

A letter that I received from Mr Arthur Nightingale of Thetford had a rather endearing twist in the last paragraph. He said in his letter, 'I am writing to ask you if you would be kind enough to give a pair of bedsocks to Miss Emily Parsons of Thetford in Norfolk. She is eighty-seven, has two broken femurs, a broken wrist from falls, Alzheimer's disease and is doubly incontinent, but she still enjoys life immensely. She used to be a good classical pianist and will still hum along with the Beethoven piano concerto or a Tchaikovsky symphony. I am seventy and she used to be my housekeeper, now I look after her. She is a lovely, sweet-natured old lady.'

With the launching of the bedsocks, a number of listeners thought that I was *appealing* for bedsocks, or was actually in need of them myself, because I received many pairs of bedsocks which had been lovingly knitted. Fortunately, I don't suffer physically from cold feet – although I have them psychologically every so often – so I sent them to homes where better use could be made of them. I have to confess though that the pair of knitted mice I received I have kept for myself.

With these letters it was possible to show the caring side of Britain. So often when people picked up their Sunday morning papers, they would see nothing but trouble. To be able to have a slot on the programme which was dedicated to those who cared for others was a real privilege and, I hope, encouraged others to be thoughtful.

There was one lollipop that wasn't quite a lollipop and it demanded a tremendous amount of work on the part of Hilary Mayo and Jenny Pitt. It was the *Good Morning Sunday Cookery Book* and I'm pleased to say it has sold like hot cakes.

Guests and listeners, as well as members of the *Good Morning Sunday* team, were asked to submit their favourite recipes, but it had to be one that tied in somehow with the Church's year. With a little bit of stretching this was achieved and as an introduction to each recipe a piece was written about the particular feast, or fast, with which it was connected. It was also good to be able to include some Jewish recipes. *Good Morning Sunday* lollipops are not always trivial but when they are serious they make every effort to sugar the pill of learning.

It was not only a one-way traffic in lollipops. Frequently I would receive gifts from listeners. There were two ladies I met in Lichfield Cathedral when I went there to do a charity

*Songs of Praise.* Every Christmas they sent me two dolls wearing exquisitely handknitted clothes for me to give away. I have in my own kitchen at home a lovely teacosy that was sent to me. It is made in the shape of a very contented cat and does faithful service when I go to the trouble of making a pot of tea, rather than just dipping a teabag into a mug.

# POSTSCRIPT

It has been a tremendous privilege to be allowed to broadcast. Not only have I met a great number of fascinating people, some of whom are internationally famous, but I have also been in touch with many who go about their day to day lives with faith, courage, love and a good deal of humour, despite the burdens that they have to carry.

Some look on the broadcasting that I do as sentimental slush, but I have always seen it as meeting people where they are, rather than where you would want them to be. But once that meeting has taken place, then hopefully you can travel on together. That seems to be the pattern that Jesus followed in his use of parables and it would be difficult to find a better communicator than Jesus.